D0586363

The Proper Care of
HAMSTERS

Marianne Mays

Photography: Bonnie Buys, Isabelle Français, Michael Gilroy, Chris Henwood, Burkhard Kahl, Horst Mayer, Lol Middleton, Susan C. Miller, and Ron and Val Moat.

Opposite page: A young Cream Hamster.

Distributed in the UNITED STATES to the Pet Trade by T.F.H. Publications, Inc., One T.F.H. Plaza, Neptune City, NJ 07753; distributed in the UNITED STATES to the Bookstore and Library Trade by National Book Network, Inc. 4720 Boston Way, Lanham, MD 20706; in CANADA to the Pet Trade by H & L Pet Supplies Inc., 27 Kingston Crescent, Kitchener, Ontario N2B 2T6; Rolf C. Hagen Ltd., 3225 Sartelon Street, Montreal 382 Quebec; in CANADA to the Book Trade by Macmillan of Canada (A Division of Canada Publishing Corporation), 164 Commander Boulevard, Agincourt, Ontario M1S 3C7; in ENGLAND by T.F.H. Publications, PO Box 15, Waterlooville PO7 6BQ; in AUSTRALIA AND THE SOUTH PACIFIC by T.F.H. (Australia), Pty. Ltd., Box 149, Brookvale 2100 N.S.W., Australia; in NEW ZEALAND by Brooklands Aquarium Ltd., 5 McGiven Drive, New Plymouth, RD1 New Zealand; in the PHILIPPINES by Bio-Research, 5 Lippay Street, San Lorenzo Village, Makati, Rizal; in SOUTH AFRICA by Multipet Pty. Ltd., P.O. Box 35347, Northway, 4065, South Africa. Published by T.F.H. Publications, Inc. Manufactured in the United States of America by T.F.H. Publications, Inc.

The Proper Care of
HAMSTERS

Marianne Mays

Approved by the British Hamster Association

To Kantarell,
the hamster that got me
into the world of hamsters.

Acknowledgments

Many thanks must go to Anne Dray for writing the chapter about genetics, and to Gerald and Vicky Coley and Sarah Pattison for supplying animals for photographs. Our thanks also to the British Hamster Association for the use of their exhibition standards.

Contents

A nice Satin Cinnamon long haired female.

About the Author

MARIANNE MAYS was born Marianne Bornhult in Sundbyberg, Stockholm, Sweden in 1966. As a small girl, she showed a keen interest in animals and longed for a pet of her own but was denied this by her parents. However, when Marianne was nine, they relented, and she acquired a cavy as a pet. This was the beginning of a long and varied lifetime of pet ownership. Marianne kept many other pets but found her true pet love when she was 13 years old and obtained her first hamster, which she "rescued" from being unwanted.

Over the next few years, she acquired many more hamsters of several different varieties and bred many beautiful specimens. She joined hamster clubs in England, where the hamster fancy originated, and learned all she could about the latest developments in the fancy. She worked as a veterinary nurse for several years. In 1982, along with a number of other interested hamster fanciers, she formed the Svenska Hamsterföreningen—the Swedish Hamster Club. The S.H.C. was incredibly successful and gained many members across Sweden and from other countries as well. Many shows were held, and several varieties of hamster developed. In 1985, the S.H.C. spawned the Swedish rat fancy and, for a time,

Marianne occupied the position of president in both groups!

Marianne moved to England in 1988 after marrying Nick Mays, the noted rat fancier. Whilst there, Marianne became a hamster judge in the British fancy and, together with Nick, was a founding member of the British Hamster Association.

Marianne Mays is a well-respected fancier, judge, and author (her first hamster book was published in Sweden in 1986), and she writes regularly for a number of magazines in England and Sweden.

She and her family—husband Nick, daughter Rebecca, and almost countless cats, dogs, rats, rabbits—and hamsters, naturally—live in Doncaster, Yorkshire.

Opposite page: A typical hamster, healthy and alert.

Foreword

No two hamster "experts" will give exactly the same advice when asked about a particular aspect of hamster care, each person building upon their individual experiences and education to produce a unique perspective on the best way to keep these entertaining pets.

Marianne Mays has amassed a vast amount of knowledge over many years of hamster keeping, and this has enabled her to include within the following pages practical advice and helpful information which few would claim to match.

The book provides comprehensive information about the care and welfare of the ever popular Syrian, or Golden, Hamster and also the newer, but increasingly popular, Dwarf Russian and Chinese Hamster species.

The book provides sound advice for the novice hamster keeper. It includes sections on purchasing a hamster, basic care and welfare, successful breeding techniques and common diseases that might be encountered. It also manages to whet the appetite of those who wish to explore in more detail the world of hamster breeding, genetics, and exhibiting, and provides useful references for those who wish to take their hobby further.

I commend this book to you.

Anne Dray
Chairman, British
Hamster Association

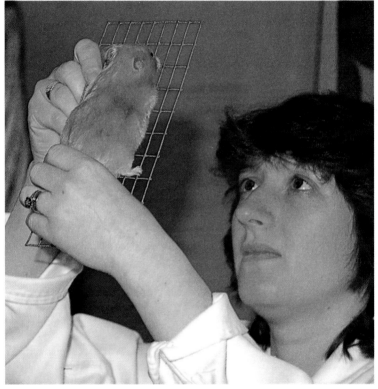

Judge Anne Dray inspecting an entry in the Satin class.

The Hamster as a Pet

Are hamsters suitable pets? The answer is definitely *yes*, but before deciding on a hamster as a pet, carefully consider the following points:

• Hamsters come in many varieties and in a few different species as well. Do you want a Syrian, or Golden, Hamster, or a pair of dwarf hamsters? Their care does differ, so it is important that you have decided on which species to get before you purchase.

• Hamsters can become very tame but are very small animals,

Opposite page: Good friends. Hamsters can make good pets for people of all ages.

can sometimes be rather lively and, therefore, difficult for young children to handle. A child of perhaps seven years of age will be perfectly capable of handling a hamster, but a younger child might be better off with a bigger pet, such as a rabbit, a guinea pig, or perhaps best of all, a fancy rat.

• Hamsters are nocturnal and, therefore, are asleep during the day. This makes them suitable pets for school children and working adults, but if you want a pet to keep you company in the daytime, a hamster may not be the best choice.

• A hamster, like any other animal, will need daily care and is not something that can be tucked away in a corner once the novelty has worn off. Are you sure you want the responsibility that a pet brings?

On the plus side, hamsters have many virtues that make them ideal pets for children and adults alike. They are cheap both to purchase and to maintain. They will live happily in a fairly small cage that will not take up too much space in your home. They do not need to go for walks, as do

A Black Eyed White Hamster. This is a beautiful but rare variety.

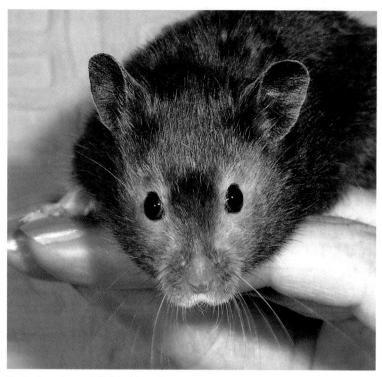

A nicely coloured Sable Hamster.

dogs. As long as the cage is kept clean, they do not smell, as they are very clean animals. They can become very tame and friendly and may even make you new friends if you decide to take up showing and breeding. In fact, the hamster's only drawback is that it is very short lived. After approximately two years its life will end; and if you have become very fond of your pet, it may be heartbreaking to lose him or her.

The Syrian Hamster

In the first part of this book, we will deal only with the most common of hamster species: the Syrian, or Golden, Hamster. The various species of dwarf hamster will be covered in the last few chapters.

The Syrian Hamster (*Mesocricetus auratus*) has been a popular pet

Long haired Satin Cinnamon Hamster.

A long haired Black Eyed Cream Hamster.

since the 1950s. It is one of the all-time favourites among the small pets. It was originally discovered near Aleppo, in Syria. The most famous discovery of the Syrian Hamster was made in 1930 by Professor I. Aharoni, from Hebrew University in Jerusalem. He uncovered a nest with 12 Syrian Hamsters, a mother and her young, and brought them back to Jerusalem. Most of them died during the journey, so Professor Aharoni was left only with two females and a male. For a long time it was said that this was the first discovery of the Syrian Hamster and also that none had since been discovered wild, but, in fact, the Syrian Hamster has been found wild both before and after this date. The latest discovery

Do not forget to fit a mesh lid on an aquarium tank that is used as a cage, or the hamster will soon find its way out.

of wild Syrian Hamsters occurred as late as 1983. It is true to say, though, that basically all Syrian Hamsters living today have the trio from 1930 as their common ancestors. Initially, Syrian Hamsters were used only as laboratory animals, but when they proved not to be very suitable for this, they were released into the pet market and that is where they have stayed.

The Syrian Hamster is only one of several species of hamster. The biggest hamster is the European Hamster, which can reach the size of a rabbit. The smallest species are the various dwarf species, such as the Russian and the Chinese Hamsters. They measure only about 7 centimetres as adults, whereas the Syrian Hamster may be up to 15 centimetres long, with an average weight of 130-180 grams for males and 150-250 grams for females.

The Syrian Hamster is a rodent, but it does not have many similarities with rats and mice, with which many people seem to associate it. The Syrian Hamster has a short, cobby body, a blunt nose and fairly large, rounded ears. It has four toes on each of its fur-covered front paws and five each on the back paws. Its tail is very short, measuring only about 1-2

Syrian Hamsters come in a variety of colours and coat patterns.

centimetres. On each hip the Syrian Hamster has a scent gland. Many people mistake these glands for wounds. The glands are sometimes black, sometimes flesh coloured. They may or may not be covered with fur. When the female hamster is in season and ready to mate, she will produce a strong scent from these glands, which attracts the male. The male also has these glands, but his do not produce any scent. He will merely lick them when he feels or smells the presence of a female in season.

Syrian Hamsters come in many coat and colour variations. They can be short haired, long haired, have a curly rex coat or a shiny satin coat. They can be the natural golden colour, white,

A Golden Dominant Spot of poor quality. A Dominant Spot should be a white animal with small coloured patches. This hamster will still make a nice pet.

Hamsters are active, agile little animals.

cream, black, grey, etc. All hamsters have cheek pouches, which are used for transporting food. A hamster will not store food in its pouches. It will put it there temporarily for safe keeping or for transportation. A female with young may even carry her babies in them. The pouches are very big compared to the size of the hamster. A Syrian Hamster can carry up to half its own weight's worth of food, which is how it got its name *hamster*. (In German and Swedish, the word *hamster* means "to hoard.") A hamster will usually designate a corner of its cage as a store area. There he will put his favourite foods, such as peanuts and sunflower seeds. It is important, when the cage is being cleaned out, to look through the hamster's store. Throw away any food that has gone off, such as vegetables, but do let the hamster keep his store of seeds, as it will upset him if it is all removed!

A Cinnamon Banded female with her one-week-old babies.

SYRIAN HAMSTER FACTS
Class: Mammalia
Order: Rodentia (rodents)
Family: Cricetidae
  (hamsters)
Species: *Mesocricetus
  auratus* (Golden, or
  Syrian, Hamster)
Average adult weight:
  Male 130-180 grams,
  Female 150-250 grams
Oestrus (reproductive
  cycle): Every 4 days

Gestation: 16-17 days
Average litter size: 5-8
Birth weight: 5 grams
Fur grows: 5 days
Eyes open: 12-14 days
Weaning age: 4 weeks
Sexual maturity: 5-6
  weeks
Reproductive life: male,
  18 months+; female,
  12 months
Life span (average): 2
  years

Selection and Purchase

WHERE DO I BUY MY HAMSTER?

The question of where to buy your first hamster is usually answered by "from the pet shop." This is often a good choice, as many shops these days stock an excellent variety of pet hamsters at a reasonable price. The pet shop can also supply you with all the equipment and food you will need. If, however, you may be thinking about showing, or you want to know your hamster's background, then it is

Opposite page: A pretty long haired male hamster. **Below:** Adult Syrian Hamsters should never be kept in pairs. In almost all cases, they will fight to death.

A long haired Sable Roan, sometimes called a Blue Roan or Silver.

wise to visit a local breeder. The different hamster clubs will be able to advise you of breeders in your area, and there may even be a hamster show that you can visit. At such events there are usually quite a few hamsters for sale, from different breeders, so you have a good chance of finding the particular variety that you want. If you want your hamster only as a pet and are not too bothered about particular colours, then your local pet shop will probably be your best and easiest choice. Just make sure that the pet shop is a good one, where the animals are looked after properly.

Hamsters make good children's pets but must be handled carefully so that they do not fall and injure themselves.

A very attractive long haired Satin Cream Hamster.

WHAT VARIETY SHOULD I CHOOSE?

The coat or colour variety that you choose is mainly a matter of personal taste. All varieties make equally good pets, and there is no difference in temperament as there is, for example, in rabbits, cats and dogs. A long haired male hamster may grow a very long coat, 10 centimetres or more, and will, therefore, require a certain amount of grooming; but this is negligible, so do not be put off a long hair for this reason. The long haired females never

An alert hamster in a state of watchful attentiveness. Note the erect ears.

grow as much hair as do the long haired males, so they need no more grooming than a short haired hamster.

WHAT SEX?

If you want your hamster for breeding, you obviously know what sex to choose. But, if all you are after is a nice pet, what sex should you decide on? Basically, both males and females can make very good pets, but there are a few slight differences between the sexes to bear in mind.

• Females can become just as tame as males, but quite often they are more difficult to tame than males. Once adult, males also tend to be more placid than females.

• A male will usually live a little longer than a female, perhaps a few more months.

• A female will come into season every four days and, when she does, she produces a fairly strong smell from her scent glands. She may not do this if there is not a male around, so

This is an ideal travelling cage for hamsters.

it may not necessarily be a problem. But if you want to make sure to get a pet with no smell, a male may be better.

THE IMPORTANT RULE

Your next question will probably be whether to get just one hamster or to get two so that they have company. The answer to this is very simple. Get *one* hamster. There is a very important rule to remember when you are dealing with Syrian Hamsters: Only one hamster per cage—never, ever, put two adult Syrian Hamsters in the same cage. Some people may argue that they have seen hamsters living together peacefully in pet shops. They may have

A litter of young hamsters enjoying their food. Pictured are a Golden, Cinnamon, Cream, and Golden Banded.

A basic but good type of hamster cage. The water bottles that are attached to the sides of the cages are an excellent means of administering water to the occupants.

friends that have kept a pair of hamsters together for years without any problems. My advice is to forget all of this. In at least 99% of all cases, two adult hamsters will fight to death. The only time you can leave two adult hamsters together is during the few hours when the female is in season. Adult hamsters *will* fight, and they do not stop until one of them is dead. Because of this, hamster babies will have to be separated at five weeks of age, at the latest.

Some particular strains of Syrian Hamster will live together happily for a few months, but most do start to fight at about six weeks. The hamsters that you see living together in pet shops are, most often, youngsters less than six weeks old. Older hamsters may look peaceful during the day,

This is the correct way to hold a hamster.

A Young Golden Banded enjoying a run in his exercise wheel.

when the shop is open, but at night they become active and do start to fight. Some people do seem to refuse to accept this fact. I once arrived at a hamster show and noticed a woman who had two hamsters in each cage. She loudly explained to anyone that was interested that all her hamsters lived in pairs, and they never fought. She only split them up when showing, as the rules state that there must be only one hamster per show cage. At this particular show,

A Cream female with babies a few days old. Already their fur is growing.

I was book stewarding, so I had the opportunity to look closely at all the entered hamsters. It was very easy to recognise this woman's hamsters. They all showed evidence of bite wounds! So never forget the important rule: *only one hamster per cage—never, ever put two adult Syrian Hamsters in the same cage.* It will only end in a tragedy.

WHAT AGE SHOULD MY NEW HAMSTER BE?

Hamsters that are for sale in pet shops or from breeders are generally between four and six weeks old. This is a very good age to purchase your pet hamster, as it is young and should be easy to tame. A hamster younger than six weeks is also very unlikely to be pregnant. You can, of course, also buy an older hamster. If you want a hamster for showing, this may be a very good idea, as then you can more easily assess what the hamster will look like, both in size and type. It can be difficult to tell how well a four-week-old hamster baby will turn out as an adult. There should not be any difficulty in taming an older hamster. In fact, it may be tame already, as hamsters settle down with age and are less skittish than when a few months old. If you do buy an older hamster, however, there are two things to bear in mind. The first thing is to make sure that the hamster has been kept in a separate cage. Any female older than six weeks that has been in contact with males is likely to be pregnant. Also find out exactly how old the hamster is. As

Items such as apples and carrots make good hamster food, but they should be chopped into small pieces!

hamsters only live for approximately two years, you will lose out greatly if you buy an animal that is already a year old.

WHAT TO LOOK FOR

When selecting your hamster, you should carefully check that it appears to be in good health. If it is a show animal you are after, you should also make sure that the hamster has the particular qualities that you want, such as correct markings. A healthy hamster has bright eyes that are clean; the eyelids must not stick together. Remember that hamsters usually sleep during the day, so they may not be very alert. The fur should be soft and dense and absolutely clean. It is very important that the hamster is clean and does not have any stains, especially around the tail area, as this may be a sign of diarrhoea. The

Play houses such as this one are an attractive addition to a Syrian Hamster's cage, but they are not really necessary.

A Cinnamon Dominant Spot Hamster.

skin should be soft and clean, free from yellow or white flakes. The same applies to the ears. Some hamsters, such as cream coloured ones, may have black spots of pigmentation on their skin. This is normal and nothing to worry about. Finally, check that the hamster does not have any bite wounds. If it has, it has been kept together with its brothers and sisters for too long and, if female, may be pregnant.

HOW TO SEX A HAMSTER

How to sex a hamster correctly may take a bit of practise but is easy once you have learned how. Do not accept statements such as "I can't sex this hamster because it's still very young" from either pet shop assistants or breeders. A hamster can *always* be sexed, if you know how to do it!

The way to sex a hamster depends upon its age. Newborn hamster babies are most easily sexed by checking the distance between the vent and the sex organ. It is much greater in the male than in the female. If you compare two babies of different sexes, it is easy to see the difference. The two openings are very close together in the female. In babies approximately one week old, the female's nipples can clearly be seen in two rows on the belly. Later, when the hamster develops fur on

Opposite page: A female Syrian Hamster. Learning to sex hamsters will take a bit of practise in the beginning.

Note the comical expression on this little character's face. Hamsters can be entertaining pets.

its belly, these become more difficult to distinguish. On hamster babies about three to four weeks old, the easiest way to sex them is to use the same method as for newborn babies. The males may also have developed their testicles, which can be seen. Sexing the adult hamster is very easy. The female has a rounded bottom with the two openings close together. The male appears to be more drawn out, due to his large testicles, which can be seen clearly.

Opposite page: A male Syrian Hamster. In male hamsters, there is a greater distance between the sex organ and the vent.

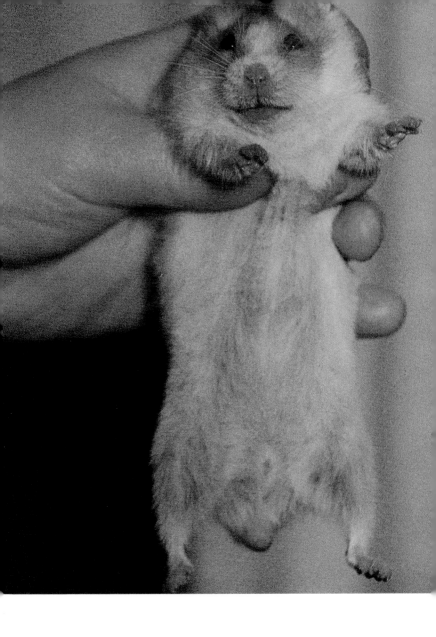

Care and Equipment

THE CAGE

There are several different types of cages available for hamsters. Most of them can be found at your local pet shop. The cage should not be smaller than 30 x 25 centimetres and, ideally, it should be tall enough to hold a large exercise wheel. The bigger the cage the better, although a hamster will live quite happily in a fairly small cage, as long as it has something to do, such as an exercise wheel to use or some cardboard tubes to chew. What must never be used are cages with several floors, or very tall cages such as

Opposite page: A Golden Umbrous Hamster amusing itself in its playball.

bird cages. Hamsters *do* love to climb, but they are fairly clumsy and can easily fall and hurt themselves. I once had a two-storey hamster cage. One evening, the hamster that lived in it fell down the ladder from the first floor to the bottom. It was not a very long fall, but the hamster landed on his head and died. I have also seen hamsters with fractured limbs and ribs, the result of injuries from the cage in which they lived.

Another type of cage to avoid is the plastic sort with several different "apartments," all connected by plastic tubes. Some of these cages can be very dangerous. They easily get too hot in the summer as the ventilation is not good enough and, as the tubes are fairly small, a very large hamster (perhaps the show type, as they often are bigger than pet hamsters) could get stuck.

The third type of cage that should never be used is a round cage.

Hamsters do not like round cages. True, they live in burrows in the wild, but in captivity they much prefer a square cage, where they can make their nest in one corner, food store in another, toilet in a third, etc.

So what is the best type of cage for a Syrian

An aquarium tank makes a perfectly suitable hamster cage.

A good type of commercially produced hamster cage. It is conveniently equipped with a self-attached exercise wheel.

Hamster? Well, the cheapest, easiest to clean out, and most practical is the usual type available in pet shops: a square cage with metal bars at the top and a plastic bottom tray. This cage is very easy to keep clean, the hamster can climb the bars if he wants to, and it looks attractive. Also, this type of cage is reasonably priced. Avoid the old-style cage with a metal base, as it can get rusty and be dangerous.

If you want a cage in

which you can see your hamster clearly but from which no sawdust or shavings can fall on the floor, an aquarium tank is ideal. This is also a very good breeding cage, as newborn hamster

A hamster with full cheek pouches. The pouches are very big compared to the size of the hamster.

babies can sometimes fall between the bars of an ordinary cage. If you do use a tank, you will have to make a wire lid that is securely fastened so that the hamster cannot escape. You will also need to construct a wire holder in which to contain the water bottle. Tanks can look very attractive, and they certainly keep clean the area in which the hamster is kept. Bear in mind, however, that they are heavy and can be awkward to clean out.

If you are handy and have the time and the proper tools, you can make your own hamster cage out of wood. Once again, you will also need to have a wire lid, as hamsters are very good at escaping and can climb out of most cages. The wood should be

A Cinnamon Dominant Spot Hamster fast asleep in its travelling cage.

treated with a non-toxic wood preserver to make sure that it does not rot.

For those who keep a lot of hamsters for breeding and showing, there are some cheap alternatives to cages. A plastic wash bowl with a wire lid makes a cheap cage that is easy to clean out, and the same goes for laboratory cages, which you can sometimes get second hand. I do not like these cages very much. Both are very low, which means that the hamster may not be able to stand up on its hind legs, and they will not hold an exercise wheel.

OTHER EQUIPMENT

The most important thing in a hamster's cage is bedding. There are several different types from which you can chose. The best type is white wood shavings. You can purchase them in any pet shop. They are very absorbent and will not cause any discomfort to the hamster. They are nice and soft, and the hamster can easily make a nest out of them. Sawdust can also be used, but this is not ideal, as it may get stuck

A Dark Grey Hamster. This colour often goes slightly brown as the animal ages.

in the hamster's eyes or nose and will not keep as clean as shavings. Nor can the hamster make a nest out of sawdust. So, if it is used, separate nesting material is necessary.

For very long haired hamsters, cat litter may be an alternative. Wood shavings and especially sawdust easily get caught in the hamster's long fur and will cause knots. The easiest way to prevent this is to groom your hamster regularly,

All of your hamster's cage accessories should be cleaned on a regular basis.

Water should always be available to your hamster. A water bottle will keep the water cleaner than will a bowl.

but if you prefer, you can use cat litter in the cage, as this will prevent the problem. It must not be white cat litter, however, as this is very dusty and can irritate the hamster's eyes. As cat litter is rather uncomfortable to sleep on, the hamster will need special nesting material.

Newspaper should never be used as bedding for a hamster because the ink is toxic and may cause allergic reactions as well as stains on the fur.

Regular cleaning out of the hamster's cage is essential. For a small- to medium-sized cage, this should be done at least once a week. A larger cage may be left as long as two weeks, as hamsters are very clean little animals. Do change the bedding in the toilet area, though. Hamsters usually use one particular corner of their cage as a toilet area, so this is easily done.

Nesting material is necessary when you use sawdust or cat litter as bedding, as described above. However, you must never use any kind of nesting material for a female with babies, as a baby can swallow some

A nice long haired Mink Banded youngster. A low-cut cardboard box does not make a safe temporary holding area: the occupant can easily jump out and injure itself.

A Cream Hamster of lovely, cobby type.

of the material and choke. There are several different kinds of nesting material available from your pet shop. The very best kind is the soft shredded paper. It is comfortable and harmless. Do not use the types that look rather like cotton wool as some of them can injure the hamster in several ways. If the hamster puts some of this material in its cheek pouches, he or she may choke to death. This material can also get

The fruits and vegetables that you feed your pet should always be of the freshest quality.

tangled around legs and cut off the blood supply, costing the hamster its leg. Do not use hay, as it can damage the hamster's eyes and cheek pouches and bring in mites.

Houses or nest boxes are neither necessary nor advisable. A hamster will easily make his own nest of the wood shavings or nesting material. A plastic house should never be used for Syrian Hamsters, as it will get too hot and may make the hamster lose some of its fur. It also takes up unnecessary space in the cage. If you absolutely do want to use a house, chose a wooden one.

A must in every hamster cage is a feeding bowl and a water bottle. Do not use water bowls, as they quickly get messy. A bottle is ideal.

Your local pet shop can supply you with a pet hamster and all the equipment that you need to care for it.

The food bowl should, ideally, be made of very tough plastic, metal, or ceramic. Soft plastic bowls will be chewed and tipped over and should be avoided.

An exercise wheel is something that many hamsters love. People may argue and say that it is cruel to let the hamster run round and round in a wheel. This is not true.

A hamster will use its wheel if it really likes it. I once made an experiment with one of my hamsters, who loved her wheel very much. I let her run free on the floor of my bedroom. In the middle of the floor I put an exercise wheel. Even though the hamster had the whole floor to discover, she chose to use her wheel instead. I personally think that the wheel is very important. It does not make the hamster too thin for showing, as some people claim. It simply gives them exercise and something to do.

There are many exercise wheels available for hamsters, and some of them are, unfortunately, not very good. Do not use plastic ones, as they will be chewed. Never use a wheel that is smaller than 13cm across, as running in a smaller wheel can seriously injure a hamster's back. Wheels with solid backs are usually the best kind, but as they are generally too small, opt for an open metal wheel.

Other toys are not really necessary. No hamster will benefit from budgie toys, such as bells and mirrors, and it may injure itself on ladders. The play balls that are available may be used but never for more than 15 minutes at a time. How would you feel if you were a hamster and were shut inside a plastic ball for hours on end? If you want to give

Opposite page: A long haired Chocolate Hamster.

An attractive Cinnamon Dominant Spot mother with her three-week-old offspring.

your hamster other toys, old cardboard tubes and boxes are the best choice. These are harmless and will give the hamster much pleasure when he chews them and hides inside them.

FEEDING

Hamsters are omnivorous, which means that they will eat almost anything, unlike, for example, the rabbit and the guinea pig, which are vegetarians. This does not mean, however, that the hamster is allowed to eat everything!

The most important thing for a hamster is always to have some sort of a "hamster mix" available. There are several good types of hamster mix obtainable from pet shops. A good one contains sunflower seeds, peanuts, flaked maize and peas, oats, wheat and pellets, or a mixture of most of these. Do not buy a rabbit mix for your hamster, as this is unsuitable. A rabbit mix does not contain enough protein for

A good type of hamster mix, containing flaked maize, crushed peas, oat flakes, sunflower seeds, peanuts, pellets, and dried vegetables.

hamsters (the hamster needs about 18%, whereas a rabbit will only need 14%), and some rabbit mixes also contain anti-coccidiosis medication, which can be harmful to animals other than rabbits.

You can also make your own hamster mix, should you prefer to do so. It may include sunflower seeds, sesame seeds, millet, plain biscuits, raisins, corn flakes and oat flakes.

The hamster should always have a bowl of hamster mix available in the cage. Every evening you top this up as necessary. Apart from the mix, the hamster will also occasionally (perhaps a couple of times a week) need supplements, such as fruit or vegetables, or perhaps potatoes, a small piece of meat, etc. Hamsters like many types of food and can sometimes eat your own table scraps, but never feed anything that has spices, such as salt and pepper, added. Neither should you give your hamster citrus fruits, as the acid in them can be damaging, and sweets such as chocolate and other candy should be avoided at all times. There are several types of hamster treats available in pet shops. Be careful with them. They are often treated with additives to keep them fresh for a long time, and some hamsters are allergic to them. Dog biscuits are good for hamsters to chew, but never give the kind that are meant to be soaked. If they are given without soaking, the biscuits will expand inside the hamster's stomach and may literally cause the hamster to burst! Cat biscuits can be given, but not too many, as they are extremely high in protein. The best choice is to buy low-protein dog biscuits or to make your own hamster biscuits. A hamster's teeth are growing all the time, so they do need something hard to chew to wear them down.

A hamster's basic diet is fairly simple and inexpensive. There are a variety of hamster mixes from which you can choose.

SUITABLE HAMSTER FOOD

Apple
Carrot
Cucumber
Lettuce
Iceberg lettuce
Cabbage
Cauliflower
Swede
Tomatoes
Banana
Pear
Grapes
Peach
Melon
Peas
Berries
Sprouts such as bean sprouts
Potato, cooked or uncooked
Dandelion leaves
Clover
Boiled Rice
Pasta
Spaghetti
Pancake
Egg
Chicken
Fish, cooked
Meat
Mealworms
Sweet corn

A young White Hamster eagerly waiting for his snack.

An exercise wheel is one of the best investments that you can make for your hamster. It will give him countless hours of enjoyment.

be approached from above. This frightens them, as this is the way they would be attacked if they were living in the wild. Therefore, always try to approach a new hamster from the side, so that he can see your hand coming and not be startled. With a very nervous hamster, it is best to cup both your hands around him and gently scoop him up. A more tame hamster can be picked up by simply placing your hand around his body just behind his legs. Do not attempt to lift the hamster by the scruff of his neck. This will not hurt him, but it does frighten him.

If you have not quite got the courage to start picking up your hamster straight away, you could make a gentler approach. Put some peanuts, sunflower seeds, or something else tasty in your hand, and tempt the hamster with them. Eventually, he will feel brave enough to take the food from your hand and will also, in time, climb onto your hand. This taming method takes longer but can be very effective.

Very young hamsters can be extremely nervous and skittish. In fact, they behave rather like popcorn: they bounce all over the place! Don't worry though...The hamster will settle with age.

Always be wary of picking up a hamster that is asleep. Hamsters do not normally bite, but a hamster that has been woken up from a nice sleep may bite out of fright. Always try to gently wake the hamster before you pick him up or, rather, do not pick him up at all if he is not awake! Obviously, at shows for example, there are times when it is necessary to pick up hamsters that are asleep. That is when it is necessary for your hamster to be really tame, so that he can be handled without problems.

HAMSTER BEHAVIOUR

What does it mean when my hamster does this and that? Here is a description of common hamster behaviour and what it means:

• The hamster is chewing on the bars of its cage, perhaps even making his mouth and nose sore by doing so. Meaning: the hamster is bored! Give him something else to chew, such as a biscuit or a cardboard tube. Males that smell a female in season may also chew the bars in an attempt to get out.

• The hamster is rubbing himself or herself against the sides of the cage, perhaps even falling over while doing so. It walks on tall legs and may make a sound not dissimilar to sneezing. Meaning: the hamster is ready for mating; it wants a mate.

• The hamster is standing tall on its hind

Give your hamster ample time to adjust to its new environment.

legs and listens carefully. He or she also squeaks. Meaning: the hamster is "talking" with another hamster in the same room. This usually happens when there is a female in season.

• The hamster is licking your hand. Meaning: this is not a show of affection for you. It merely means that your hand smells very interesting. Perhaps you have just handled a female in season or some very tasty food?

• The female hamster stands very still and stiff with her tail erect and eyes half closed. Meaning: she is in season and ready to be mated.

• The hamster is grinding its teeth. Meaning: anger, possibly fear.

• The hamster is screaming. Meaning: often fear but can also be anger, such as in a fight with another hamster. Hamster babies often scream when they play, or even in their sleep.

• The hamster is licking its hip spots. Meaning: he or she is ready for mating.

• The hamster is laying on its back, holding its paws up and opening its mouth. Meaning: "Go away, you have disturbed me and I'm not in a good mood!"

THE HAMSTER AND OTHER ANIMALS

Can you keep hamsters with other animals? The answer is yes, but you must be careful. Hamsters generally do *not* mix with other animals. It has been known for hamsters to make friends with other animals, but this is rare and is not something with which you should experiment. I once had a hamster that moved in with a pregnant mouse. When the mouse had her kittens, the male hamster shared care with the mouse! This was something truly amazing, and I do not think that I will ever see anything quite like it again. All the other hamsters that I have kept—and these number several hundred—have always killed any mice with which they have come into contact. Here is a list of other common pet animals and how they are likely to behave with a hamster in the house.

Cats: Cats are predators, and most cats will kill hamsters, even those cats that are permanently kept indoors. It is vital, therefore, that you keep your hamster in a perfectly escape-proof cage. Even better is to keep the hamster in a closed room to which the cat has no access.

Dogs: Some dogs will accept and even like hamsters; others will kill them, and some are not interested at all. Never take a chance. Keep the dog and the hamster apart. A dog can, of course, also be taught that it must not touch the hamster, even if it is outside its cage, something that is not possible with cats.

Rabbits: Rabbits are usually not bothered by hamsters at all, nor does the rabbit interest the hamster.

Guinea pigs: Much the same as rabbits.

Mice: Mice that come into contact with hamsters will usually end up being eaten by the hamsters, so beware.

Rats: Rats are predators, just like cats, and even the tamest one will kill a hamster given the chance. Keep them

A nice specimen of the Cinnamon variety.

well apart.

Gerbils: Will fight with the hamster, so keep them well apart.

Birds: Small birds will probably not be interested in the hamster, and vice versa. However, parrots may be a danger so do not let them near the hamster.

Basically, always keep your hamsters separate from other hamsters and other animals. This does not mean, however, that you cannot keep both hamsters and other animals. All it takes is some careful planning. My husband and I keep, apart from hamsters, several dogs, cats, rabbits, guinea pigs, birds, mice, gerbils, chinchillas, and rats.

Breeding Syrian Hamsters

So you want to breed hamsters? Before you actually go ahead and do so, sit down and think the prospect through, thoroughly. Why do you want to breed? Do you want a litter from your pet "just for fun," or do you want to go into serious breeding, with showing in mind? Most important of all: do you know how to find new homes for the babies? A Syrian Hamster can have anywhere from one to over twenty babies (although the average is around eight), and these will need either to be sold or housed singly by the time they are five weeks old. If you cannot find homes for the babies, you may find yourself with an extra ten or so cages! So, consider the matter carefully before you let your hamsters breed. Keep in mind that it's not always possible to give the hamsters away to people who'll care for them well, and it's even less likely that you'll be able to sell them. As regards selling hamsters, incidentally, don't expect to make a great profit out of hamster breeding, because you won't.

SELECTING THE FEMALE

If you have only one pet female that you want to breed from, then, obviously, you will not have any difficulty choosing your female. Do make sure, however, that she is fit for breeding.

She should be approximately four months old and certainly not older than eleven months at the time of her first litter. She should be of a good size and be in good general health. Remember that temperament as well as looks is passed on in breeding, so do not breed from a female that is very nervous or very aggressive.

Do not breed from a female that is more than 12 months old, even if it is not her first litter. Females older than this seldom or never manage to rear a litter. Some just do not get pregnant, some do get pregnant but become ill and lose the litter, and some give birth to weak babies that do not survive. It is not worth the risk; let the female retire as soon as she is a year old. In the same way, do not breed from a female that is younger than three months, as she will not be sufficiently mature and will still be growing. Only mate her as early as three months if she is of exceptionally good size. Do not confuse good size with being fat: a fat female is not likely to conceive. She must be fit.

If you intend to breed hamsters for showing, you will probably have a few females to chose from. Pick the one that most closely resembles her breed standard. A slightly mismarked female may very well be able to produce offspring that are better marked than she is, especially if mated to a well marked male, and the same applies, to some extent, to colour. Do not expect

Hamster babies start eating solid food at just over one week of age.

large, well-typed babies from a small female of poor type. Always breed from the best that you have. Breeding from poor-quality animals will not bring success on the show bench.

SELECTING THE MALE

The male you select should also be in good general health and match your requirements if you are breeding for showing. Males can usually mate as young as five weeks of age, but such an early mating does not always result in a litter. Some males are not even interested in females until they are three to four months old.

You can use the male for breeding for about 18 months, provided that he is fit. Do not use a male older than this, as the strain of mating may be too much for his heart.

COAT VARIETIES

After the selection of colour, the final thing to consider when choosing which two hamsters to mate together is the coat. The different coat varieties of the Syrian Hamster are as follows: short haired, long haired, satin, and rex. The satin gene can be combined with both that of rex and long haired, so that you could, for example, have a long haired satin rex. Rex can be found in long haired, short haired, and

A pretty ten-day-old Black Hamster with its White littermates.

A long haired Cream female with her three-week-old youngsters.

satin varieties, and satin can be found in all the different varieties. Generally, for the best results, you mate a short haired to a short haired and a long haired to a long haired, even though it is possible to mix the two breeds without ending up with mongrel hamsters.

The rex gene is recessive, so to get rex babies you must either mate two rexes together or one rex and a rex carrier—that is, a normal coated hamster that has one rex parent. The satin gene is dominant, and you should always mate a satin coated hamster to a normal coated hamster. Do not attempt to mate two satins together. The result will be "double satins": hamsters with a double dose of the gene, and they are not pretty. Their fur is sparse and greasy and nothing like the ordinary shiny satin coat.

INBREEDING

Inbreeding is mating together two closely related animals, such as brother to sister, father to daughter, etc.

Many people shudder at the thought of inbreeding. They have visions of related individuals that are being bred together, producing weak, perhaps even deformed, offspring. This is simply not true. Inbreeding does not create any faults, it simply brings out qualities that are already present—good or bad. Inbreeding can be very useful, but you must know what you are doing. If you just go ahead and mate together two closely related animals without knowing their background, you will most likely end up with small, weak animals. Any defect that is hidden, perhaps even generations away, will come to light with inbreeding. It is essential, therefore, that you make sure that the animals you inbreed do not carry any faults.

On the other hand, if

The result of a mating between two Roan Hamsters: an eyeless White Hamster.

your hamsters have a particularly *good* quality that you wish to preserve, such as very good size and type, inbreeding is the best way to "fix" this into your strain. Almost all the best show animals of one species or another are inbred to a certain extent. Often, you can tell who bred a particular animal just by looking at it. With careful inbreeding, you can create a stud of hamsters that all look very similar, which is the idea behind it all. You want all the hamsters that you breed to be good enough to show, not just one every now and then. The breeders that are turning out consistently good show animals are no doubt using inbreeding. Of course, inbreeding can go too far, and you are likely to need an outcross from an unrelated or partially unrelated strain sooner or later.

LINEBREEDING

Linebreeding is usually the best method and is certainly the best for beginners, as it does not involve mating together such closely related animals as is required with pure inbreeding. Linebreeding can, for example, mean mating a female back to her grandfather, mating two cousins together, or a half-brother and sister.

THE MATING PROCEDURE

Mating two hamsters together is not as simple as it may seem. You

When the female is ready for mating, she stands completely still with her tail raised stiffly.

Before and after the mating, the male will wash both the female and himself.

cannot just put the male and female together for a few days and wait for them to mate, as is usual with guinea pigs, for example. Nor can they live together permanently, as is common with mice and gerbils. The female Syrian Hamster will accept the male only when she is in season. At any other time she will attack him and may badly injure him or even kill him. It is vital, therefore, that you find out when she is in season.

The female comes on heat every four days. She only comes on heat in the evening, and it will be later in the summer than in the winter because of the length of the day. Remember that hamsters are nocturnal! In the winter, the earliest time to mate a female is usually around 8pm. In the summer, it may be as late as 10pm before she comes on heat. Her season usually lasts through the night.

The first step to check as to whether or not the female is in season is to take her out of her cage and put her in a neutral area, such as on a table (but do make sure that she cannot fall off) or a fenced-off area on the floor. Let her walk around and gently scratch her back. The chance is that she then will go into the mating position. She will freeze, standing with her tail erect and eyes half closed, ready for the male. If she does this, fetch the male and let him get on with his business.

Not all females are this easy, though. She just may not react to your hand. If she does not, you will have to fetch the male and let him find out whether she is on heat. The male will sniff the female's rear and attempt to lick her. While he does this, scratch her back to encourage her even more. If she is on heat, she will now get into the mating position. If she is not, she will turn on the male, so you must remove him immediately to avoid a fight. A female that shows the slightest interest in the male, such as sniffing him, is likely to attack any second, so remove the male quickly. If she really is on heat, she will just freeze and not want to investigate the male at all. If the worst should happen and the female does attack the male, it is

Normal Golden female Hamster with her babies. They are approximately two weeks of age.

vital that you separate them quickly, or the male will be badly injured. It is a good idea to have a towel handy, which you can throw over the hamsters. You can also use a piece of wood or a book to separate them. Do not attempt to separate them with your bare hands, as you will probably get bitten.

If the female is not in heat, separate the pair and try again the next evening. If you try four evenings in a row, you are bound to hit the right evening eventually.

If all is well, the hamsters will mate. The male will lick the female and perhaps pull her around a bit to get her into a better position. He will then mate her several times and wash both himself and her in between. The female will remain still. If you sit and watch them the whole time, you can leave the hamsters on the table or the floor, or wherever you first put them. If not, put them together in the male's cage. *Never* put them in the female's cage, as she may attack the male to defend her home, even if she is on heat. Let the hamsters mate for about fifteen minutes and then put them back in their respective cages. The female will now "come to life" and start washing herself.

IS THE FEMALE PREGNANT?

Has the female become pregnant? This can be a very difficult question to answer. One method is to again try her with the male four days after mating. If she is not on heat, you can assume that she is pregnant. This is not always true, however, as some females have false pregnancies, rather like dogs, and actually think that they are pregnant when they are not.

If the female is pregnant, and if she is having a large litter, it may be possible to see after ten to twelve days that she has become fatter. If the litter is a small one, she may look almost the same as normal all the way through the pregnancy, and you will not know for sure if she is pregnant until she is actually due, which is after 16 or 17 days. If nothing has happened after 17 days, the mating has failed, and you must start all over again.

PREPARATIONS FOR THE BIRTH

As you will not know for sure whether or not the female is pregnant, it is best to assume that she *is* and so prepare for the birth. The first and most important thing to do is to make sure that the female is in a suitable cage. Her normal cage may not be ideal for breeding. If she is in a cage with bars, the bars must be very close together, about ½

A litter of Sable and Banded Sable Hamsters, about ten days old. They will open their eyes in a few days' time.

centimetre apart, or a baby may fall out of the cage between the bars. You can buy cages with "mouse bars," which are close together, or cages with a deep bottom tray, and these are ideal. An aquarium with a fine mesh lid is also very good for this purpose.

When the female has a litter, she should have wood shavings in her cage. She will make a comfortable nest out of them for the babies and herself. Do not use

A Cream female Hamster and her litter. The youngsters are approximately four weeks old and are ready to leave home.

A Dark Golden Banded Hamster. The band should cover about one-third of the hamster's body and must be unbroken.

sawdust, as it can get inside a baby's mouth and suffocate it. Nesting material of any kind is not recommended for the same reason.

Clean out the female's cage a day or so before she is due to give birth. It is important that the cage is clean when the litter is born, as you will not be able to clean it for about two weeks afterwards. If she has a wheel, it may be a good idea to remove it. This will ensure that the babies are not injured in it, whether by running in it themselves when old enough, or by their mother's using it. Many females tend to build their nest right behind the wheel.

The female does not really need any special food supplements when she is pregnant, but if you like, you can give her potatoes and milk to ensure that she develops plenty of milk. Otherwise, it is not until the babies are born that you need to start feeding more than usual.

Make sure that the female's cage is in a good location. You do not want it close to a window, as this may be either too cold or too warm for her. You do not want it in a place where people are coming and going all the time, as this will worry the female. Put the cage in a quiet place where the female can give birth in peace. A female that is disturbed, either when giving birth or later, may kill and eat her litter to "protect" it.

THE BIRTH

The female Syrian Hamster is pregnant for only 16 or 17 days, which is one of the shortest gestation periods known in any mammal. The most natural time for the female to give birth is during the evening, but birth can take place at any time during the day. It is perhaps most usual for the female to give birth during the night of the 16th day, so that when you wake up on the 17th morning, the litter is there.

It is not difficult to tell when the female is getting ready for the birth. She will run around her cage and scratch in every corner, trying to decide which is the best place for her nest. This may go on for several hours.

Eventually, she will settle down and build a deep nest in her chosen spot. Sometimes she can

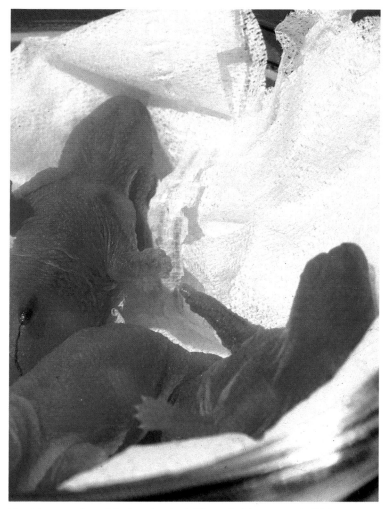

Hamsters are born blind and naked. These babies are only thirty minutes old.

be completely covered by shavings. When she has got this far, leave her in peace. The very best thing is to leave the room. It is essential to make sure that she is not disturbed during or after the birth, as this may make her kill the babies. Do not play loud music anywhere in the house or use the vacuum cleaner nearby, as the sounds will disturb the female. Make sure that no other animals, such as cats or dogs, are present. If the female is a very tame pet, she may accept your presence. In that case, you can sit quietly by the cage, and watch and listen. You may see the babies born, or you may see nothing at all if the

A Cream female and her young, which are about ten days old. The gestation period for a hamster can range from 16 to 17 days.

female is well covered in the nest.

The female will give birth to her babies one by one, and it is a remarkably quick procedure. She will clean each baby as it is born, and as soon as the baby has been washed, it will start to suckle. All in all, it may take about an hour for a hamster to give birth to a litter of ten or so. Any babies that are born dead or die soon after birth for some reason will usually be disposed of by the mother: she will eat them. This is perfectly natural and nothing to worry about.

When the female has given birth, she will be very reluctant to leave her nest. It may be difficult, therefore, to tell whether she has actually had the babies or not.

Sure signs are usually a few blood stains just outside the nest, and if you listen carefully, you can hear the babies squeak. If you want to see the babies, perhaps to be able to count them, try to tempt the female out of the nest for a minute with some tasty food. She will probably be hungry after having given birth and will appreciate it. She may cover the babies up as she leaves the nest. If so, uncover them carefully by parting the woodshavings, but under no circumstances must you touch the babies. The female will most likely not accept your scent on them.

IF THE FEMALE HAS DIFFICULTIES GIVING BIRTH

Sometimes things go wrong, and you may find

that the female cannot give birth to her litter. If a baby obviously is stuck and part of it can be seen, you must help her by removing it gently. Once the obstructing baby has been removed she can usually give birth to the rest with no further problems.

If the female is obviously pregnant but nothing has happened after 17 days, see a vet. He may be able to induce her and, with luck, the babies will be born alive.

These Sable youngsters are about two and one-half weeks old. Their colour will turn more brown than black as they grow older.

Any female that has not given birth after 18 days is either not pregnant or her babies are dead. If she carries dead babies she may start to bleed, and again you need to see a vet. The hamster will need an injection to get the babies out, or she will die. Afterwards, it is most likely that she will also need a course of antibiotics. It is more or less impossible to perform a Caesarean section on a hamster. Even if a good vet were able to do the operation and get the babies out alive, it is most probable that the female would not look after them.

IF THE FEMALE DIES

If you are really unlucky and your female dies, you are left with a big problem: a litter of babies, perhaps newborn. If they are younger than 10-14 days, it is virtually impossible to save them.

Whereas animals such as guinea pigs and rats will accept other females' babies, a hamster will not usually accept any young other than her own. One out of a hundred may accept strange babies, but usually it is not even worth trying. If the female does not accept the strange babies, she may well kill and eat both them and her own litter.

If the motherless babies are about two weeks old, it may be worth trying to handrear them. To handrear babies younger than this is very difficult, but once they have reached this stage, they will start to take solid food as well as milk and it is worth trying.

A Satin Silver Grey Hamster. Note the lovely sheen of the coat.

Buy a milk substitute from your pet shop, and feed it to the babies. Use a syringe or eye dropper if they will not lick from a plate or bowl. Also buy soft baby food and offer it to the babies. With luck the litter will survive. Remember, though, that they will need feeding several times a day at this age, not only once or twice.

DEFORMED BABIES

Very occasionally a female may give birth to a baby or babies that are in someway deformed. It may have a deformed leg, for example. Usually the female will instinctively kill any babies that she knows are not healthy, but, if you do find yourself with a deformed baby, it is probably best to have it put down. It can be hard to tell how badly deformed the baby will be as an adult. A deformed leg, for example, may not cause a young, lightweight hamster any problems, whereas it can be a great handicap to a large adult.

CARE OF THE MOTHER AND BABIES

During the first 24 hours after the female has given birth, you should leave her alone, in peace. Feed her by all means but do not attempt to examine either the babies or her, as this will disturb her. As well as possibly killing her babies, even the tamest female may try to bite you if you interfere with her newborn young which, after all, is only natural.

When the babies are three days old, you can remove the female from the cage for a moment and examine the babies. Count them and, perhaps, sex them. Before you attempt any handling of such young babies, rub your hands in some of the female's soiled shavings. This way your hand will carry the female's own scent. Do not clean out the cage for at least ten days. You can remove any heavily soiled bedding in the toilet corner, but under no circumstances must you interfere with the nest. If you clean the cage out completely, the mother will be very worried on her return. She will probably pick her babies up and run around with them in her mouth, searching for her nest. A really nervous female may even put her babies inside her cheek pouches. This is very dangerous, as it may cause the babies to suffocate. If your female should start to behave like this, for whatever reason, put her cage in a very quiet spot and cover it with a blanket or a towel to make it dark. Usually the female will then soon settle down.

THE BABIES' DEVELOPMENT

Baby hamsters develop very quickly. When they are born, they are naked, deaf and blind. They are completely pink, and you can see no trace of any colour. The only thing you can tell at birth is their sex and their eye colour. A black eyed baby will have dark patches where the eyes will develop, whereas a red or ruby eyed baby will have the same colour all over

Hamsters are adept climbers as evidenced by this hamster "working out" in his cage.

the body. At birth, the babies already have tiny teeth, but it will obviously be a while before they can use them. The babies' tails appear fairly long in contrast to the rest of the body at this stage. After 24 hours, the teeth have already grown bigger, and if any babies are going to be dark coloured, you can begin to see that the skin is getting a little bit darker. The babies will also start to crawl around on their bellies, whereas during the first day they could only lay on their backs. On the third day, the babies will have developed small whiskers and are covered in very fine fur. It is now more easy to see whether the babies are going to be pale or dark, self coloured or marked, as the pigmentation of the skin becomes more obvious. On the fourth day, the babies' ears will start to unfold, although they will still not be able to hear anything. After five or six days, the babies may want to start eating solid food. Very often you will find a baby happily chewing away on its mother's droppings! At this stage, you can sprinkle some oat flakes or other soft cereal over the nest for the babies to eat. After a week, the boldest babies may try to leave the nest, but, if they do, their mother will soon retrieve them and carry them back. On the eighth day, it is very easy to sex the babies, as the females will have two distinct rows of nipples on their bellies. The males have nipples as well, but they are much more faint. After fourteen days, most babies will start to open their eyes (although some may take a day or two longer), and

At five weeks of age, the male and female members of a litter should be separated to prevent mating. Additionally, each hamster will need its own accommodation; otherwise, fighting is sure to ensue.

this is also when they will want to leave the nest. The female may try to put them back in the nest to start with, but she will soon give up. It is now safe to clean out the cage. The babies will now have fur all over, but it is still not possible to tell whether they will be long haired or short haired. This takes another week or two. They are now able to hear, but their ears are still slightly folded. They will unfold fully by the age of three weeks. At the age of three weeks, the babies will weigh about 30-60 grams and look more like miniature adults. They will want more and more solid food, so do make sure that there is always plenty available. Baby food, cat food, bread, and vegetables are ideal to give them. At the age of four weeks, the babies will be fully weaned, and they should now be separated from their mother. She will probably be more than fed up with them and will be happy to get the cage back to herself. At five weeks of age, the males must be separated from the females to prevent mating, and at six weeks all the babies must have single accommodation or they will start to fight.

Possibly you will now have less babies than at the birth. This is not unusual. It is very common for perhaps three or four babies to die during the first few days or that the female may reduce the number herself if she feels that she cannot cope with a big litter. If after the first litter has been weaned you want to mate the female again, I recommend that you let her rest for about a month first. She will have worked hard bringing up her babies and will probably have lost some weight. She will need time to recover before she has to go through it all again.

WHY DOESN'T MY FEMALE GET PREGNANT?

Sometimes a mating fails. Why? Well, that is not always possible to answer. If the female has not become pregnant, try again. If the mating fails the second time, sit down and have a think about things. Is the female at the right age for breeding? If she is 12 months or older, it is likely that she will have become infertile. Is she in

A three-day-old hamster.

good enough condition?

It may help to give her vitamin E supplements a few days before the mating. What time of year is it, and what is the temperature? Hamsters do not normally breed during the winter months. If they are kept indoors in a centrally heated house, they will usually breed without any problems all year 'round, but hamsters that are kept in a cold room, or perhaps in a shed, will not usually breed during the winter. Are you sure that the male is fertile? Occasionally you do come across sterile males. Try another one and see if you have better luck. Bear in mind that all *ruby eyed* males are sterile after the age of ten weeks! If nothing at all seems to work, the reason may be that the female herself is sterile. Luckily this is not very common.

This is a rather unusual variety of the Syrian Hamster: the Rex. This is a long haired Satin Rex in Red Eyed Cream.

Genetics

BY ANNE DRAY

Most people recognise that there are similarities between parents and offspring, but it is also noticeable that they differ in many ways. The science of genetics attempts to explain the processes that lead to these variations. An organism's inherited characteristics are determined to a greater or lesser degree by the transmission of information from parents to offspring during reproduction. It is now known that this information is contained in structures called *genes*, which are grouped together in *chromosomes*. The number of chromosomes varies between species. For example:

species	chromosomes
man	46
horse	64
house fly	12
Golden Hamster	44

The specific genetic makeup of an organism is termed its *genotype*, which determines its appearance, physiology and behaviour.

The appearance of an organism is called the *phenotype*, and it is changes to the phenotype that are immediately noticeable to the breeder and for which genetic explanations are normally sought. The wild, or naturally occurring, organism exhibits a phenotype that has evolved through natural selection of those organisms best suited to the local environment. Behind this phenotype is a genotype that "guarantees" the production of offspring also ideally suited to the normal habitat. However, the genotype of an organism can alter through *mutation* (change) of the genetic material.

It is not possible to cover the cause and process of mutation in this book. Suffice it to say that mutations do occur, and where these changes occur, there can be a significant visible change in the phenotype of an organism (for example, its coat colour). Other changes may be less obvious, such as changes in the number of teeth, but may also affect the way an organism interacts with its environment and hence its ability to survive. For example, a mutation changing a rabbit's coat colour to white would be an obvious advantage if it lived in snowy climes, but not in a forest, when it would be much more visible to predators. By convention, these mutations are given standard symbols, which are used to convey information to the breeder.

Some characteristics are inherited in a *dominant* way, i.e., are visible in an animal receiving the gene from only one parent. These genes are shown by the use of a capital letter, e.g., Lg. Other characteristics are inherited in a *recessive* (hidden) way, i.e., are not visible if inherited from only one parent. These genes are shown by the use of a small letter, e.g., e. Animals receiving only one dose of a dominant or recessive gene from their parents are said to be *heterozygous* for the gene, or are *heterozygotes.* If recessive genes are inherited from both parents, then the characteristic will show in the appearance of the offspring. If dominant genes are inherited from both parents, then the effect of the dominant genes in the double dose can be quite distinct from the action of the dominant genes in a single dose. Animals receiving two doses of a dominant or recessive gene from their parents are said to be *homozygous* for the gene or are *homozygotes*. The Syrian Hamster has a number of recorded mutations, primarily affecting the coat colour and coat type. Documented mutations to date are listed below, together with brief descriptions of the phenotypes. Colour mutations in the Syrian Hamster are often classified into agouti patterned or self coloured. The agouti pattern is the pattern of the wild Syrian Hamster: it appears as a dark dorsal colour tipped with dark hairs and a uniform greyish colour at the base of the coat, a pale whitish belly colour and darkly pigmented cheek flashes. The self colour tends to have a uniform colour over the whole surface of the animal, with only slight lightening of the colour on the belly or down the length of the hair.

COLOUR MUTATIONS

genetic symbol	genetic name	common name	agouti(a) self(s)	description		
				coat	ears	eyes
a	black	black	s	black	black	black
b	brown	rust	a	rust	dk. grey	black
c	dark eared albino	dark eared albino	s	white	black	red
dg	dark grey	dark grey	a	grey	black	black
e	non extension of eumelanin	black eyed cream	s	rich cream	black	black
f	frost	frost	a	dilute	normal	pink
J	jute	jute	s	pale orange	light grey	black?
Lg	lethal grey	light grey	a	beigy gray	black	black
p	pink eyed	cinnamon	a	orange	brown	dk. red
ru	ruby eyed	ruby eyed fawn	a	fawn	brown	ruby
Sg	silver grey	silver grey	a	pale grey	dk. grey	black
T	tawny	tawny	a	dilute	?	?
To	yellow	yellow	a	yellow	black	black
U	umbrous	sooty golden	a/s	dark brown	black	black

To many hamster fanciers, the prospect of developing new colour varieties is one of the most exciting aspects of the hobby.

PATTERN MUTATIONS

genetic symbol	genetic name	common name	description
Ba	white band	banded	Band of white fur encircling the midriff. Often broke along the dorsal line.
Ds	dominant spot	dominant spot	White spots over the dorsal surface of the animal, white belly fur, ruby eye or eyes.
Mo	mottled	mottled	Mixture of normal and white hairs.
pi	pinto	pinto	Large areas of white spotting, white belly fur, dilute pigmented areas.
s	piebald	piebald	White spots over the dorsal surface of the animal, white belly fur, ruby eye or eyes.
Wh	anophthalmic white	white bellied	In heterozygotes, the belly fur of the animal is pure white to the roots in agouti patterned. In self colours, the colour is heavily sprinkled with white hairs. Homozygotes are normally white and eyeless (eyeless whites).

COAT MUTATIONS

genetic symbol	genetic name	common name	description
hr	hairless	hairless	The animal has no fur.
l	long haired	long haired	Females have 1.5cm-length fur, males have up to 8cm-length fur.
N	naked	naked	The animal has no fur.
Sa	satin	satin	Coat has a very glossy sheen.
rx	rex	rex	Whiskers and coat are wavy/frizzy.

The preceeding tables include most of the genes documented to date in the Syrian Hamster. Breeders can, however, create new colours or *varieties* by combining two or more colours, patterns or coat types in one animal. For example, combining cinnamon (pp) with dark grey (dgdg) would give a lilac (ppdgdg).

To illustrate how breeders can increase the numbers of different genotypes, or create new colours, several breeding schedules are shown below. Firstly breeders need to become conversant with breeding terminology. A breeding programme is normally shown thusly:

parent x parent
↓
first generation   F1
offspring
↓
second generation   F2
offspring

The second generation is produced by crossing brother and sister of the

A Cinnamon Hamster. This animal is too pale: the colour should be richer.

first generation (F1).

To take a simple cross of golden (the wild type—genotype normally depicted as ++) x the black eyed cream (ee):

First cross
parents   golden (++) x cream (ee)
results in F1   all (+e), i.e., golden phenotype but
                 heterozygous for cream

Second cross
F1 x F1   i.e., +e x +e
results in F2   25%++, i.e., golden phenotype
                 50%+e, i.e., golden phenotype but
                 heterozygous for cream
                 25% ee, i.e., cream phenotype

This cross is better explained using a layout called a Punnett square.

First Cross

	parent +	+
parent		
e	+e	+e
e	+e	+e

Second Cross

	parent +	e
parent		
+	++	+e
e	+e	ee

By the use of this method, many combinations can be predicted prior to the actual mating taking place, and breeders can make the best crosses to maximise their chances of producing new varieties. The following table shows many of the new colours that can be created by combining the current mutations available in the Syrian Hamster.

COLOUR VARIETIES

genotype	variety	description		
		coat	**eyes**	**ears**
ppdgdg	lilac	pale lilac grey	dk. red	dk. grey
bbdgdg	beige	dark lilac grey	black	dk. grey
ToTodgdg	smoke pearl	ivory	black	black
ppee	red eyed cream	rich cream	red	grey
ppToTo	honey	pale orange	red	grey
UUee	sable	sable/black	black	black
UUeebb	chocolate	chocolate	black	black
ppLg+	blonde	creamy/grey	dk. red	grey
eedgdg	black eyed ivory	ivory	black	black
eedgdgpp	red eyed ivory	ivory	dk. red	grey
eeruru	ruby eyed cream	pale cream	ruby	flesh
UUeeDs+	silver	white with sprinkling of black hairs	black	black

Naptime for a sleepy hamster.

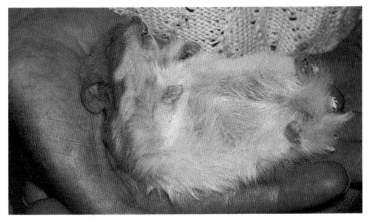

A section of the author's hamstery. Storage space, ventilation, lighting, and temperature control are important factors when setting up a hamstery.

The Hamstery

A stud of hamsters is called a hamstery. A hamstery can be either small or large. A small hamstery may only include perhaps two males and five females, whereas a large hamstery can include several hundred hamsters. The main reason for keeping this many hamsters is obviously to breed seriously with showing in mind.

When you breed a lot of hamsters, it is extra important that you keep the hamsters in a place where the mothers will not be disturbed. The hamsters in their cages should be easy to get to, and the cages should be easy to clean out. You will want to keep as many hamsters as possible in the minimum amount of space, and you want the room where they are kept to be easy to clean. It is not practical to try to breed hamsters in a front room full of furniture and with a fitted carpet. You will need a space somewhere that is only for the hamsters (and possibly other small animals such as gerbils, if you keep more than one species).

THE ANIMAL ROOM

One good place to keep your hamstery is in a special animal room. This is what I prefer and use. An animal room does not need to be a specially constructed room. A spare bedroom will do very well. An attic room or a basement may do nicely as well, but remember that it is very important that the room does not get too cold in the winter or too hot in the summer. It must be well ventilated, and there must be daylight, so a window is essential.

The room you use as an animal room must be escape proof, should any hamster get out of its cage. For example, there must not be any gaps under the door. There must not be any electrical cables that the hamsters can get to. You do not want a carpet on the floor, as it only gets messy. It is also necessary to have good lighting in the room.

The most important thing in the animal room is good shelving. You can put your hamster cages on these shelves, which saves a lot of space. The top shelves can be difficult to get to when feeding and so on, so save them for storing such things as show pens. Somewhere in the room you will need to store food and, perhaps, shavings as well. A dust bin is ideal for this purpose. Another essential piece of equipment is a broom, so that you can sweep up shavings from the floor. A table and a chair are very useful.

Keeping hamsters in an animal room is ideal, as it will be easy for you to feed them and clean out the cages. As the temperature indoors is likely to be warm, even during the winter, you will be able to breed your hamsters all the year 'round.

There are many types of storage shelves that will enable you to keep a large number of hamster cages in a small space.

THE SHED

Many hamster fanciers keep their hamstery in a shed. This may be your only option if you do not have a spare room in your house. A shed can work very well, and it will certainly keep all the wood shavings out of your home; but it does involve more work than keeping your hamsters indoors.

As in the animal room, you will need shelves in the shed for the cages. You may be able to nail or screw shelves straight onto the wall and so save on the cost. Never put any cages with hamsters in on the top shelves, as the heat will come through the roof in the summer; on a hot summer day hamsters living on a top shelf may easily get heat stroke and die.

For the same reason, it is important that you put curtains on the shed windows so that you can cover them when it is hot and sunny. You will also need a screen door for the spring and summer. It is fairly easy to make one yourself by using wood panels and fine mesh. When the screen door is fitted, the shed will be well ventilated, and the hamsters will get plenty of fresh air, but no stray cats or dogs will be able to get inside.

As in the animal room, you will probably want to have a table and a chair — if the shed is big enough — a broom, and a dust bin for food storage. The bin that you use in the shed must be made of metal and have a tightly fitting lid. If it does not, the food may attract wild mice and rats, and you certainly do not want them among your hamsters, as they can spread disease.

There are some negative points in keeping your hamsters in a shed. It may be difficult to fit lighting, and you will have to feed the hamsters early during the short winter days — before it gets dark. It will be more awkward for you to mate hamsters, as it will mean going out to the shed at night. And, finally, as a shed is

A very nice Black Hamster.

bound to be fairly cold in the winter, most hamsters kept in a shed will not breed during the winter months.

RECORD KEEPING

When you breed hamsters it is important that you keep accurate records. When you keep several hamsters, it is very easy to forget, for example, the age of a particular hamster or who its parents were. When breeding with particular colours in mind, it is important to know what colours the hamsters have in their pedigrees, or the breeding result may not be quite what you expected.

All hamster breeders have their own particular ways of keeping their records, and, no doubt, you will find a way that suits you. The following description is how I keep my records, in a way that seems to work well for me.

To begin with, it is important to label each hamster cage. It may seem impossible to mix up two hamsters but, when your numbers start to grow and you have several hamsters of the same colour, it is all too easy to forget which hamster is which. All you need is a small sticky label showing the hamster's name on the front of each cage. I use a blue pen for males and a red one for females.

The second important thing is to keep a pedigree for each hamster. You may not always know a particular hamster's ancestors or even its parents, especially if you acquired it from a pet shop or at a show, but do write out a pedigree anyway, with the details that you do have. A pedigree should include the hamster's name, sex, date of birth, coat variety, colour, breeder or place of purchase and then, of course, its parents, grandparents and perhaps also littermates. The best place to keep all your hamster pedigrees is in a ring binder. If you keep each pedigree in a clear plastic pocket, it will not get soiled or torn. When a hamster dies, you note the date of death on the pedigree.

Apart from the binder with pedigrees, I also use a box file for my hamsters. In it is a card

PEDIGREE For: <u>SYRIAN HAMSTER</u> Date of Birth: <u>17/10 1990</u>   Sex: <u>FEMALE</u>

Breed: <u>LONGHAIR</u>   Colour: <u>DARK EARED WHITE</u>   Number: <u>—</u>

Studname: <u>LUCINDA</u>   Name: <u>LUCINDA'S WHITE WEDDING</u>

PARENTS	GRAND – PARENTS	G. G. – PARENTS	G. G. G. – PARENTS
SIRE LUCINDA'S NO NAME Longhair Light Grey Banded OWNER: M. Mays	**SIRE** LUCINDA'S CHARLIE COTTON Shorthair Satin Dark Eared White	**SIRE** LUCINDA'S DORIAN S.H. Golden dom. spot	S. LUCINDA'S SOFT SNOWBALL S.H. Cream dominant Spot D. LUCINDA'S DELIGHTED SATIN MIST S.H. Satin L. Grey Tort
		DAM LUCINDA'S DELIGHTED SATIN- MIST S.H. Satin Light Grey Tortoiseshell	S. ZOOMIX'S DUNDER S.H. Satin Yellow D. MOONACINDY MIXED DELIGHT S.H. Light Grey
	DAM LUCINDA'S JUST GREAT Shorthair Light Grey Tortoiseshell/White	**SIRE** BARNSLEY Shorthair Yellow Banded	S. NOT KNOWN D. NOT KNOWN
		DAM LUCINDA'S MUCH BETTER L.H. Light Grey Banded	S. LUCINDA'S TYPICAL S.H. Normal Gold Banded D. STERLING SILVER L.H. Light Grey Banded
DAM LUCINDA'S WILL DO Shorthair Satin Light Grey Tortoiseshell and White OWNER: M. Mays	**SIRE** LUCINDA'S CHARLIE COTTON Shorthair Satin Dark Eared White	**SIRE** LUCINDA'S DORIAN S.H. Golden dom. spot	S. LUCINDA'S SOFT SNOWBALL S.H. Cream dominant Spot D. LUCINDA'S DELIGHTED SATIN MIST S.H. Satin L. Grey Tort
		DAM LUCINDA'S DELIGHTED SATIN- MIST S.H. Satin Light Grey Tortoiseshell	S. ZOOMIX'S DUNDER S.H. Satin Yellow D. MOONACINDY MIXED DELIGHT S.H. Light Grey
	DAM LUCINDA'S JUST GREAT Shorthair Light Grey Tortoiseshell/White	**SIRE** BARNSLEY Shorthair Yellow Banded	S. NOT KNOWN D. NOT KNOWN
		DAM LUCINDA'S MUCH BETTER L.H. Light Grey Banded	S. LUCINDA'S TYPICAL S.H. Normal Gold Banded D. STERLING SILVER L.H. Light Grey Banded

Dick & Marianne Mays

Signed by breeder: <u>Marianne Mays 24/11 1990</u>

A hamster pedigree kept by the author. Keeping pedigrees will serve as an invaluable reference as you progress in the fancy. Try to record as many of the key details as you can for each of your hamsters.

for each hamster. When a hamster dies I remove the card, so the file is always up to date. This is also a good place to put any prize cards won at shows.

The cards are kept in alphabetical order, and each records details about the hamster, such as name, coat variety and colour, sex, date of birth, breeder, parents, and then records of litters bred from that particular hamster.

The final thing that I feel is important is to keep a book with notes of all litters bred. Here you note down the parents of each litter, including their coat and colour, when the litter was born, how many babies were born and how many survived, and then a list of all the babies in the litter, complete with a note of the name of the pet shop or person they were sold to, if you did not keep them yourself.

PAGE FROM A LITTER RECORD BOOK

Litter 70. Lucinda's Tryfan (LH Golden Umbrous) X Lucinda's Cowslip (SH Cinnamon Dominant Spot). Date of birth: 3/3/1991; 10 babies born, 10 survived.

1. Lucinda's Dark Crystal M. LH, Black Eyed White. Kept.
2. Lucinda's Moreta F.SH, Chocolate. Owner: Nick Mays.
3. Lucinda's Henbane F.SH, Sable Roan. Kept.
4. Lucinda's Promise F.SH, Sable Roan. Kept.
5. Not Named. F.LH, Sable Roan. Sold to pet shop.
6. Not Named. F.LH, Sable Roan. Sold to pet shop.
7. Not Named. F.LH, Cinnamon Umbrous. Sold to pet shop.
8. Not Named. M.LH, Mink Dominant Spot. Sold to pet shop.
9. Not Named. M.SH, Cinnamon. Sold to pet shop.
10. Not Named. M.LH, Cinnamon Dominant Spot. Sold to pet shop.

A Honey Hamster, a less common variety.

RECORD CARD

HENBANE-Female.
Date of birth: 3/3/1991.

Short haired, Sable Roan.

Sire: Lucinda's Tryfan (LH Golden Umbrous).

Dam: Lucinda's Cowslip (SH Cinnamon dom.spot).

Bred by: M. Mays.

LITTERS:

Ten babies to Delight (SH Light Grey), 9/9/1991.

A long haired Cream baby. In Cream Hamsters, the colour often darkens with age.

Health Care for the Syrian Hamster

Hamsters are fairly hardy little creatures, and with any luck your pet will not become ill during its short lifetime. There are, however, a number of diseases that hamsters can suffer from, and it can be very useful to know about them. The important rule is to always consult a vet if you are not sure about something. Do make sure that you find a vet that knows about hamsters, though, as not all do. Something very important to know is that hamsters appear to be allergic to certain antibiotics, such as penicillin, linomycin and erythromycin. Therefore, avoid using them.

THE MOST COMMON AILMENTS IN THE SYRIAN HAMSTER
Colds

Cause: Hamsters are very sensitive to draughts and sudden drops in temperature. It is always best to keep them at general room temperature, approximately 18-22°C. It is also possible for a hamster to catch cold germs from humans, so avoid handling your hamsters if you have a cold. Symptoms: The hamster is sneezing and has a discharge from its eyes and nose. It is probably lethargic, with a staring (i.e., fluffed up) coat and half-closed eyes. It will huddle in a corner and may feel cold to the touch. Treatment: A cold must be treated immediately or the cold may lead to pneumonia, which will kill the hamster. The hamster's cage should be placed in a warm and draught-free area, for example, close to a radiator. If no radiator is available, try putting a desk lamp right above the cage to keep it warm. Give the hamster plenty of nesting material. Mix one part of milk with one part of water, add a teaspoonful of honey, and give it lukewarm to the hamster. If the hamster is not noticeably better within a couple of days, see a vet.

Constipation

Cause: Usually lack of wet food, such as fruit or vegetables. It can also be caused by lack of exercise, as this can cause muscular problems. Symptoms: Distended belly, arched back, lethargy. The hamster may find it uncomfortable to move and will not like to be touched. Treatment: If the hamster still wants to eat, give it plenty of wet food, such as lettuce. If it does not want to eat, feed it a few drops of corn oil, medicinal paraffin or olive oil, using a syringe or eye dropper. This usually works very well. When the hamster is feeling better, remember to give it more greens in the future.

Discharge from the Eyes

Cause: The hamster may have been kept in a draught (such as near a window), it may have something stuck in the

Long haired normal Golden youngster. Your hamster's behaviour can be a good indicator of how the animal is feeling.

eye, it could be allergic to something, or it could have the beginning of a cold. Symptoms: A discharge from one or both eyes. The eye lids may be stuck together and will not open, particularly after sleep. Treatment: In old hamsters, this may be a sign of old age and cannot be treated successfully. Just bathe the eyes with lukewarm, slightly salty water, using a piece of cotton wool to gently ease the eyes open. If the problem has occurred in a younger hamster, try to find the cause. If there is a foreign body in the eye, such as a piece of sawdust,

Being transported can be an unsettling experience for many kinds of pets, including hamsters. Take this into account when acquiring your new pet.

An inquisitive young Cream Hamster.

carefully remove it. You may have to use a pair of tweezers or bathe the eye with water, applied with cotton wool. With serious eye infections, see a vet, who will give the hamster some eye ointment to be administered at least twice a day for a few days. In very rare cases, hamsters may suffer from entropion. This is when the eyelids are rolled inwards, causing the lashes to touch the eye, which obviously is very uncomfortable. This

Regularly check your hamster for any physical abnormalities that may develop. This includes teeth and claws, as well as the rest of the animal's body.

Pet shops stock special health and grooming products for hamsters.

condition is very difficult to treat in such a small animal, but ointment may help to make life easier for the hamster. No hamster with entropion should be bred from, as this condition could be inherited. Eyes that have been injured, for example, in fighting or on a sharp piece of hay (if it is used as bedding), will often become very swollen and dry. Part of the eye may even fall out after a while. Healing is usually quick, and the hamster will be perfectly capable of living with only one eye. Blind hamsters are very rare but can occur. Eyeless hamsters, white hamsters that are born with no eyes (from two parents carrying the eyeless gene), do also occur. These hamsters can live fairly normal lives as pets, providing their cages are always kept the same. For example, do not move a wheel or a bowl as this will confuse the hamster.

Heat Stroke

Cause: Hamsters are very susceptible to heat stroke. Make sure that the hamster's cage is never kept in direct sunlight or too close to a radiator or a fire. The hamster should always have drinking water available. Symptoms: The hamster appears to be lifeless, as if it is in a deep sleep. The fur may be wet. Treatment: It is vital to act quickly. Pour cold water over the hamster. This should revive it. When the hamster is awake again, make it drink. If the hamster doesn't seem fully recovered, see a vet.

It may need medication to prevent kidney failure.

Allergy

Cause: Hamsters can be allergic to certain items, such as food or bedding. Very often such allergies are inherited. Symptoms: 1) Sneezing, discharge from the eyes. The hamster is otherwise healthy and is not huddled in a corner as in the case of a cold. 2) Slight fur loss, flaky and dry skin, white flakes on the ears and often around the eyes. 3) Red, swollen feet. Treatment: 1) The hamster may be allergic to its bedding. This is especially common if sawdust is used. Change the type of bedding. Hamsters can also react in this way if their owner is smoking or wearing strong perfume. Try to find the cause of

A normal Golden Hamster.

the allergy. 2) Possibly the hamster is allergic to some kind of food. Change to a low-protein diet, i.e., no meat or fish (such as found in dog or cat food), no sunflower seeds or peanuts, no commercial hamster treats. Give cooked rice, white bread, vegetables, fruit and corn flakes. This type of allergy can be difficult to treat, and it may be difficult to find exactly what the hamster is allergic to. 3) Change the bedding. Never use newspapers as bedding, as the ink can cause this sort of irritation.

A Satin Golden Dominant Spot Hamster of poor quality.

The hamster's cheek pouches are mainly used for transporting food.

Wounds and Abscesses

Cause: Most often, fights between hamsters. Treatment: Clean the wound or abscess and disinfect it. Hydrogen peroxide (3% strength) is ideal for this purpose. Your vet can also give you suitable liquids and ointments. In the case of an abscess, this must be emptied and kept clean every day until the infection is gone. In very bad cases the hamster may need antibiotics, so see a vet.

Heart Disease

Cause: Usually a sign of old age, possibly an inherited weakness. Symptoms: The hamster is obviously tired and gets exhausted very easily. It may even "faint" after using the exercise

Exercise wheels may prove too stressful for the older hamster. Use common sense in this regard.

wheel. Its paws and mouth may have a blue tinge. Treatment: The hamster must be kept calm and quiet. Take the exercise wheel away from the hamster and do not let it out for a run outside its cage. It may be a good idea to change the cage to an old aquarium tank, to prevent the hamster from climbing on the bars. In the case of males, do not use them for mating. A female with a weak heart should obviously not be bred from either.

Broken Limbs

Cause: Very often a fall. Treatment: A hamster with, for example, a broken leg is usually not very bothered by this. The limb will heal itself in time, although it does not always heal perfectly straight. It is impossible to put plaster

A Light Grey Hamster sitting prettily.

on such a small animal to prevent this from happening. However, do prevent the hamster from moving about a lot until the limb has healed. Put it in a small cage or tank with no exercise wheel.

Lack of Fur and the Presence of Sores on the Inside of the Legs

Cause: Most often caused by the hamster using a non-solid exercise wheel and putting its legs through the bars, thereby

rubbing off the fur.
Treatment: Change the
wheel to a solid one if
you can find one that is
large enough (at least 13
centimetres across). If
not, dress the non-solid
wheel with paper on the
outside. This is easily
done, and when the
paper becomes soiled it is
easy to change it.

Fungus Infections
   Cause: Can be picked
up from another animal.
Can also be caused by
the hamster using a
small, plastic nest box or
house. Such houses can
often get too warm, which
causes condensation and
ultimately the
development of fungal
growths. Symptoms:
Yellow flakes on the skin,
which is very dry. The

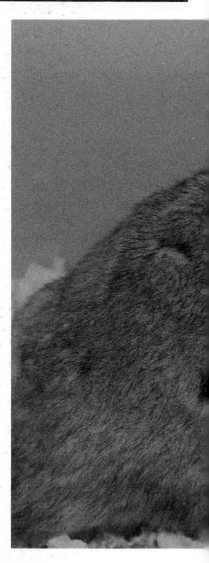

A hamster filling its cheek
pouches with food, which it will
take back to its nest.

hamster may lose fur and may be itching. Treatment: Bathe the affected areas with an anti-fungal remedy. Your vet can give you one. Iodine is also very good for this. In very bad cases, oral medications may be needed, so see the vet.

Diarrhoea
   Cause: Usually overfeeding with green food. Can also be caused by a sudden change of diet. (For other causes, see "Wet Tail".) Symptoms: Obvious loose droppings or runny diarrhoea. Both the hamster and the cage

A lovely long haired Pale Eared White male.

Feed green food in moderate amounts only: overconsumption can result in diarrhoea.

are getting very dirty. Treatment: Give only dry food until the hamster is better. In really bad cases a few drops of liquid charcoal (or a charcoal tablet dissolved in water) will usually help. Arrowroot, preferably in the form of biscuits, can also help. After a few days, gradually change back to the hamster's normal diet, perhaps with less green food supplements.

Back view of a Cinnamon Hamster.

Blood in the Urine

Cause: Usually kidney failure. Sometimes this occurs if the hamster has been fed on a lot of pellets or with food treated with antifungal remedies. Can also occur in old hamsters for no obvious reason.
Symptoms: Obvious discharge of blood. Sometimes seen as a red tinge to the urine, sometimes as pure blood.
Treatment: It is impossible to cure kidney failure, but the hamster can be made to feel better with sulphonamide medication. See a vet.

Malocclusion (Teeth Problems)

Cause: Old age usually. May also be inherited. If the hamster chews the bars of its cage, it may break one of its teeth and so allow the remaining teeth to grow too long.
Symptoms: The hamster appears hungry but cannot eat. In severe

cases, there may be a discharge of blood from the nose or mouth, where the overgrown tooth or teeth are puncturing the flesh. Treatment: Use a very sharp pair of nail scissors or wire cutters. It is not difficult to do this, but make sure that you do not injure the hamster's tongue. If in doubt, ask a vet for help.

If the hamster finds it hard to chew, feed it soft food such as baby food. Feeding it milk and potatoes as a supplement will add extra calcium to the diet, which is necessary to promote tooth growth. As malocclusion can be genetical, do not breed from any affected hamsters.

If your pet's teeth become overgrown, they will require clipping. If you are hesitant about performing this procedure yourself, ask your vet for assistance.

Overgrown Claws

Cause: Very common in old hamsters. Treatment: Use a small pair of nail clippers or scissors to trim the claws. Take care not to cut the quick, although if this happens the hamster seldom loses a lot of blood, as the blood vessels in the claws are so tiny.

"Wet Tail"

Cause: This condition is caused by a bacteria called *Escherichia coli*. It can be transferred between hamsters and often appears if the cages are not kept sufficiently clean. It is essential to keep your hamster's cage clean. Symptoms: Very bad diarrhoea, like liquid, causing the hamster's tail

Note the sharp definition of a hamster's claws. In older specimens, the claws can become overgrown and impede activities like picking up food.

Considering their small size, hamsters are fairly hardy little animals and are not overly demanding when it comes to keeping them in good health.

to be constantly wet. The hamster will probably become thin and dehydrated. If left untreated, the hamster will eventually die. Treatment: See a vet. Antibiotics will be necessary if the hamster's life is to be saved. Make sure to keep the animal warm and encourage it to drink. Lukewarm water with glucose in it is very good.

Hibernation

Cause: The hamster has been kept in too cold an environment. Symptoms: The hamster is cold and lifeless and may at first appear to be dead. Its heart is beating very slowly. Treatment: If you find an apparently dead hamster that has been kept in a cold place, such as in a shed during the winter, do not immediately give it up as dead. Carefully warm it up by placing it near to a radiator or fire. Unfortunately, it is sometimes impossible to bring 'round a hamster that has gone into hibernation, and the hamster may die.

Falls

Cause: Young hamsters often leap about a lot and it can easily happen that one falls onto the floor. Always take great care when handling hamsters. Treatment: The hamster will probably be suffering from shock. Put it back in its cage and give it lukewarm water with glucose. Leave it in peace and quiet. If it shows serious symptoms such as bleeding from the nose or is not able to

Long haired Lilac Hamster.

The life span of a hamster averages about two years.

Old Age

A hamster usually lives for around two years, but this can vary: some hamsters may die at 18 months, others may keep going for two and a half or three years. Usually, female hamsters have a slightly shorter lifespan than males.

The old hamster will start to become tired and will not move around as much as usual. It may stop using its exercise wheel. It may sleep a lot. This is only to be expected. Old hamsters may suffer from heart disease, so it is best to let them have a peaceful life. Do not attempt to use the male for breeding purposes; it will put too much strain on his heart.

An old hamster will often become thinner, the colour of the fur will become paler, and the fur

walk straight, contact a vet. Unfortunately, it may not be possible to save it if, for example, it has brain damage.

A Sable Hamster at play.

itself will start to thin out. The claws may start to grow or wear down completely. The eyelids may stick together after sleep. Strangely, some long haired hamsters may actually develop a very long, good coat at an old age.

The female hamster will usually not age in quite the same way as the male. She may appear just as usual and be in good condition until one day she suddenly dies. The male will usually slowly deteriorate during the course of a few months.

If the hamster is in poor condition, maybe becoming ill, and obviously is not enjoying life any more, it will have to be put to sleep. It is far kinder to put the hamster to sleep than to leave it to suffer for perhaps weeks.

Euthanasia

When the day comes for the hamster's life to end, it is important that this is done in a proper way. The very best way of having a hamster put to sleep is to take it to the vet. The vet will give it a lethal injection. The hamster will not feel anything and will quickly just fall asleep. When a hamster needs putting down, it is not always possible to get to the vet. The best way to put down a hamster yourself is to use chloroform. Always keep this substance at home in case you need it. Put the hamster inside a plastic airtight container and soak a piece of cotton wool with chloroform. Put this inside the container and close the lid tightly. Leave the hamster inside for at least twenty minutes. The hamster will fall asleep within seconds and, after a short while, the heart will stop beating. Always check afterwards that the heart has stopped. Feel with your finger just underneath the elbow on the hamster's left front leg.

Never attempt to drown a hamster. Its cheek pouches will fill up with

air, and it will be a very long and distressing experience for the hamster.

A lovely long haired Satin Dark Grey washing itself.

A typical hamster show in England. Attending shows will provide you with an excellent opportunity to familiarize yourself with what constitutes a good specimen of hamster. Additionally, you will meet people who share similar interests and who can be helpful as you start out in the hamster fancy.

Showing the Syrian Hamster

Why show hamsters? Well, that is a question only you yourself can answer. You may like to show your hamsters to get other people's opinions about them or to see how well you have done in your breeding programme. You may like to show hamsters because you like competitions. Or you may simply like a nice, cheap hobby where you will meet other people with the same interests as yourself. All sorts of people show hamsters, young and old, rich and poor. It is a very good way to make new friends, whatever your reason for wanting to show the hamsters in the first place. Everyone is welcome at hamster shows. You do not even need to have a show-quality hamster to enter. You can enter your favourite pet, bought from the local pet shop, in the pet class. There it will be judged only on condition and tameness, and it does not matter whether or not it conforms to a particular standard. As the hamster is a comparatively new pet, hamster shows also are fairly new. Rabbit and mouse shows, for example, have been organised since the 1800s. The very first hamster show was staged in England, in December 1945. Like most livestock fancies, the British were first to form hamster clubs and stage shows, to be followed later by countries such as America and Scandinavia. Today, hamster shows are a regular occurrence. In England, it is usually possible to show hamsters as often as once each month in your own area — and even more often if you travel around the country. In America, hamster shows are more sparse, but they are increasing and are set to become just as popular.

THE IDEAL SYRIAN HAMSTER

Hamsters all over the world are judged from a standard. The standards may vary slightly from country to country, but they were all originally based on the British standards. I feel, therefore, that it is most practical to describe the

A Yellow Hamster in the Any Other Color (AOC) class.

This Silver Grey has been bred from one Silver Grey and one Golden parent. This mating is not recommended as the golden influence makes the color too red. It is difficult to distinguish between a Silver Grey, like this one, and a Light Grey.

British standards. The standards and rules of clubs change from time to time, and what you read here may be slightly different from the rules of your local club. The standards were up to date at the time of the writing of this book, however, and they will do very well as a guide, as it is not likely that they will change greatly. If you join a hamster club, in whatever country you live, you will be given a copy of that country's most up-to-date standards.

Judging a nicely coloured exhibit in the Cinnamon class.

Not all hamsters make show animals. There are many points to consider. The hamster must be large but not fat. It should have a broad head. The fur and the colour should conform to the relevant coat and colour standard. The following is the official exhibition standard for Syrian Hamsters, as laid down by the British Hamster Association, April 1992.

SYRIAN HAMSTER SHOW STANDARDS

Type (25 points): The body shall be broad and cobby. The head shall be large in proportion to the body, with a broad skull, short face and blunt nose. The head shall be well set into the body, the profile showing a smooth curve from nose over head, to nape of neck.

Fur (20 points): The fur shall be soft and very dense. Special attention shall be paid to the density of the belly fur. In short haired hamsters the fur shall be very short and even. In long haired hamsters allowance must be made for sex, i.e., males must have longer fur than females. Matting will be heavily penalised.

Size (10 points): The hamster shall be as large as possible but not too fat. Allowance shall be made for sex, i.e., female hamsters are, in general, larger than males.

Condition (10 points):

A long haired Satin Red Eyed Cream. The satinisation greatly enhances the colour.

A nicely typed Pink Pearl Hamster—the Red Eyed variety of the Smoke Pearl.

The hamster shall be fit, alert when well awake, and tame to handle. The flesh shall be firm with no surplus fat. The coat shall have a healthy sheen, and the hamster shall be clean and show no obvious sign of injury.

Eyes and Ears (5 points): The eyes shall be large, prominent and widely set. The ears shall be whole, large, rounded, set well apart and carried erect and unfolded when the hamster is awake.

(Please note that all reference to colour of fur, eyes and ears is so far omitted.)

Colour and Markings (30 points):

Eye colour: The following sequence of eye colours shall apply in increasing order of darkness: 1. Bright pink 2. Red 3. Claret red 4. Claret 5. Ruby 6. Garnet 7. Black.

For patterned hamsters, 15 points shall be allocated for colour and markings and 15 points for pattern.

Where base colour is indicated, this applies to the whole animal.

Agouti Varieties

BEIGE (bbdgdg)

TOP COAT:	Soft pale grey with brownish tone carried approximately one-third of the way down
BASE COLOUR:	Mid grey
BELLY FUR:	Ivory
CRESCENTS:	White
TICKING:	Lightly and evenly ticked with dark brown
CHEST BAND:	Brown
CHEEKFLASHES:	Brown
EYE COLOUR	Black
EAR COLOUR:	Very dark beige

BLONDE (Lglgpp)

TOP COAT:	Creamy blonde carried approximately one-third of the way down
BASE COLOUR:	Light grey
BELLY FUR:	Ivory
CRESCENTS:	Ivory
TICKING:	Absent
CHEST BAND:	Creamy blonde with orange tone
CHEEKFLASHES:	Light grey
EYE COLOUR:	Claret red
EAR COLOUR:	Flesh with grey tone

Note: Tends to have orange tinted muzzle.

CINNAMON (pp)

TOP COAT:	Rich russet orange carried approximately one-third of the way down
BASE COLOUR:	Slate blue
BELLY FUR:	Creamy ivory with blue undercolour
CRESCENTS:	Ivory
TICKING:	Absent
CHEST BAND:	Rich russet orange
CHEEKFLASHES:	Brown
EYE COLOUR:	Bright claret red
EAR COLOUR:	Flesh with brown tone

DARK GOLDEN (++) (Wild Type Agouti)

TOP COAT:	Rich dark mahogany red carried approximately one third of the way down
BASE COLOUR:	Dark slate grey
BELLY FUR:	Ivory with grey undercolour
CRESCENTS:	Ivory
TICKING:	Heavily and evenly ticked with black — face to be swarthy with black eye rings
CHEST BAND:	Rich dark mahogany brown
CHEEKFLASHES:	Black
EYE COLOUR:	Black
EAR COLOUR:	Dark grey, almost black

A nice entry in the Golden class. This particular hamster is a Dark Golden.

LIGHT GOLDEN (++) (Wild Type Agouti)

TOP COAT:	Light fawny gold
BASE COLOUR:	Slate grey
BELLY FUR:	Ivory
CRESCENTS:	Ivory
TICKING:	Absent
CHEST BAND:	Light fawny gold
CHEEKFLASHES:	Dark grey, almost black
EYE COLOUR:	Black
EAR COLOUR:	Grey

DARK GREY (dgdg)

TOP COAT:	Pearly grey carried approximately one-quarter of the way down
BASE COLOUR:	Dark slate grey
BELLY FUR:	Ivory with grey undercolour

CRESCENTS: Ivory
TICKING: Heavily and evenly ticked with black — face to be swarthy with black eye rings
CHEST BAND: Very dark slate grey
CHEEKFLASHES: Black
EYE COLOUR: Black
EAR COLOUR: Dark grey, almost black

LIGHT GREY (Lglg)
TOP COAT: Buttermilk carried approximately one-third of the way down
BASE COLOUR: Dark slate grey
BELLY FUR: Buttermilk with grey base colour
CRESCENTS: Pale buttermilk
TICKING: Heavily and evenly ticked with dark grey, almost black
CHEST BAND: Dark brown / grey
CHEEKFLASHES: Dark grey, almost black—not solid but concentrated ticking
EYE COLOUR: Black
EAR COLOUR: Dark grey
Note: Tends to have a buttermilk tinge on face around eyes and muzzle and on sides of body.

HONEY (ppTo male, ppToTo female)
TOP COAT: Light cinnamon orange to the roots
BASE COLOUR: Light cinnamon orange
BELLY FUR: Ivory

Syrian Hamsters in their show pens.

CRESCENTS: Ivory
TICKING: Absent
CHEST BAND: Light cinnamon orange
CHEEKFLASHES: Cinnamon
EYE COLOUR: Claret red
EAR COLOUR: Flesh with grey tone

LILAC (dgdgpp)
TOP COAT: Soft pale grey with pink tone
BASE COLOUR: Soft pale grey
BELLY FUR: Ivory
CRESCENTS: Ivory with pink tone
TICKING: Absent
CHEST BAND: Soft pale grey with pink tone
CHEEKFLASHES: Mid grey with lilac tone
EYE COLOUR: Claret red
EAR COLOUR: Pinkish grey

RUST (bb) (GUINEA GOLD)

TOP COAT:	Rich orange brown
BASE COLOUR:	Mid slate grey
BELLY FUR:	Ivory with pale grey undercolour
CRESCENTS:	Ivory
TICKING:	Lightly and evenly ticked with brown
CHEST BAND:	Deep rust brown
CHEEKFLASHES:	Deep rust brown
EYE COLOUR:	Black
EAR COLOUR:	Dark grey

SMOKE PEARL (dgdgToTo male, dgdgToTo female)

TOP COAT:	Pale greyish cream to the roots
BASE COLOUR:	Pale greyish cream
BELLY FUR:	Pale ivory
CRESCENTS:	Pale ivory
TICKING:	Heavily and evenly ticked with black
CHEST BAND:	Pale greyish cream
CHEEKFLASHES:	Black — not solid but concentrated ticking
EYE COLOUR:	Black
EAR COLOUR:	Dark grey

YELLOW (To male, ToTo female)

TOP COAT:	Rich dusky yellow carried well down
BASE COLOUR:	Creamy ivory
BELLY FUR:	Ivory

A Rust Hamster, also known as the Guinea Gold.

CRESCENTS: Ivory
TICKING: Heavily and evenly ticked with
                  black
CHEST BAND: Rich dusky yellow
CHEEKFLASHES: Black — not solid but
                  concentrated ticking
EYE COLOUR: Black
EAR COLOUR: Dark grey
*Author's note: Both Yellow and Smoke Pearl will,
                  when mated to a different colour,
                  produce Tortoiseshell.*

Self Varieties

SABLE (UUee)

TOP COAT:	Black carried well down
BASE COLOUR:	Creamy ivory
BELLY FUR:	Black
CRESCENTS:	Absent
TICKING:	Absent
CHEST BAND:	Absent
CHEEKFLASHES:	Absent
EYE COLOUR:	Black-ringed with fine creamy hairs
EAR COLOUR:	Dark grey, almost black

COPPER (UUeebbpp)

TOP COAT:	Rich copper to the roots
BASE COLOUR:	Rich copper
BELLY FUR:	Rich copper
CRESCENTS:	Absent
TICKING:	Absent
CHEST BAND:	Absent
CHEEKFLASHES:	Absent
EYE COLOUR:	Garnet
EAR COLOUR:	Light brownish grey

BLACK EYED CREAM (ee)

TOP COAT:	Deep rich sandy cream to the roots
BASE COLOUR:	Deep rich sandy cream
BELLY FUR:	Deep rich sandy cream

Perhaps the most exciting newcomer of Syrian Hamsters: the melanistic (or true) Black. This variety is thought to have originated in France.

CRESCENTS:	Absent
TICKING:	Absent
CHEST BAND:	Absent
CHEEKFLASHES:	Absent
EYE COLOUR:	Black
EAR COLOUR:	Dark grey, almost black

RED EYED CREAM (eepp)

TOP COAT:	Deep rich pinkish cream to the roots
BASE COLOUR:	Deep rich pinkish cream
BELLY FUR:	Deep rich pinkish cream
CRESCENTS:	Absent
TICKING:	Absent
CHEST BAND:	Absent
CHEEKFLASHES:	Absent
EYE COLOUR:	Claret red
EAR COLOUR:	Peach grey

BLACK EYED IVORY (eeLglg or eedgdg)

TOP COAT:	Pale greyish cream to the roots
BASE COLOUR:	Soft pale greyish cream
BELLY FUR:	Soft pale greyish cream
CRESCENTS:	Absent
TICKING:	Absent
CHEST BAND:	Absent
CHEEKFLASHES:	Absent
EYE COLOUR:	Black
EAR COLOUR:	Dark grey, almost black

RED EYED IVORY (eeLglgpp or eedgdgpp)

TOP COAT:	Soft pale greyish cream to the roots
BASE COLOUR:	Soft pale greyish cream
BELLY FUR:	Soft pale greyish cream
CRESCENTS:	Absent
TICKING:	Absent

The Rust should not be confused with the similar-looking Cinnamon. This Rust has good deep black eyes, whereas a Cinnamon's eyes are dark red.

CHEST BAND:	Absent
CHEEKFLASHES:	Absent
EYE COLOUR:	Garnet
EAR COLOUR:	Light pinkish grey

DARK EARED WHITE/ALBINO (cdcd)

TOP COAT:	White to the roots
BASE COLOUR:	White
BELLY FUR:	White
CRESCENTS:	Absent
TICKING:	Absent
CHEST BAND:	Absent
CHEEKFLASHES:	Absent
EYE COLOUR:	Red
EAR COLOUR:	Very dark grey, almost black

FLESH EARED WHITE/ALBINO (cdcdpp)

TOP COAT:	White to the roots
BASE COLOUR:	White
BELLY FUR:	White
CRESCENTS:	Absent
TICKING:	Absent
CHEST BAND:	Absent
CHEEKFLASHES:	Absent
EYE COLOUR:	Red
EAR COLOUR:	Flesh

Patterned Varieties

DOMINANT SPOT (Dsds)

1. The Dominant Spot shall have the appearance of a white animal with coloured spots. The spots shall be sharply defined and evenly distributed over the top surface of the animal. The belly fur shall be white.

2. The white areas shall be white to the roots.

3. The coloured spots shall conform to the recognised corresponding full coloured variety.

4. Eye Colour: as for the full coloured variety, also ruby/red eye or eyes permissible.

5. Ear Colour: as for the full coloured variety, also flesh or partly flesh coloured permissible.

WHITE BANDED (BaBa or Baba)

1. The White Banded animal shall have the appearance of a coloured animal with a superimposed white band. The white band shall completely encircle

A Cinnamon Dominant Spot Syrian Hamster.

the body and be centrally placed and not skewed. The width shall be approximately one third of the body length, completely unbroken with sharply defined parallel margins. The belly fur shall be white.

2. The white areas shall be white to the roots.

3. The coloured areas shall conform to the full

colour variety.

4. Eye Colour: as for the full colour variety, also ruby/red eye or eyes permissible.

5. Ear Colour: as for the full colour variety, also flesh or partly flesh coloured permissible.

TORTOISESHELL AND WHITE (TotoBaba,TotoBaBa or TotoDsds)

1. A Tortoiseshell and White is a tri-coloured animal that consists of a balanced pattern of coloured, yellow and white patches. These patches shall be clear and distinct with no brindling.

2. The coloured areas shall conform to the full colour variety whilst the yellow shall be a rich creamy yellow when in combination with the golden, but shall be present in a diluted form when combined with other recognised colours. The belly fur shall be white. For example:

main colour	yellow
golden	rich creamy yellow
dark grey	smoke pearl
cinnamon	honey

3. Eye Colour: as for the full coloured variety, also ruby/red eye or eyes permissible.

4. Ear Colour: as for the full coloured variety, also flesh or partly flesh coloured permissible.

Coat Varieties

LONG HAIRED

1. The colour and markings shall conform to the recognised standard allowing for a dilution of ticking on Agouti varieties.

2. The fur shall be soft and very dense and evenly long over the top

Long haired males should have long fur all over their bodies, including their backs. This hamster is a trophy winner in England.

surface of the body, excluding the face, where it shall be shorter. In general, males shall have longer fur than females, and allowances should be made.

SATIN

1. Colour and markings shall conform to the recognised colour standard, allowing for satinisation.

2. The fur shall be soft and dense and have a glossy sheen.

REX

1. The colour and markings shall conform to the recognised colour standard, allowing for the rex coat, which will dilute

colour slightly.

2. The coat shall be soft and dense and evenly frizzy.

3. The whiskers shall be curly.

NON-STANDARD COLOURS

From time to time new colours appear, either accidentally or by having been created. If enough fanciers work on them, they may be included in the official standard at a later date. Until then, they can only be exhibited in the non-standard class at shows. In that class the hamsters are not being judged on colour. The following are examples of colours that, at present, are classed as non-standard. This is by no means a complete list.

PINK PEARL — A red eyed version of the Smoke Pearl, with paler ears and lacking the black ticking. It is produced by combining Smoke Pearl, Dark Grey, and Cinnamon.

MINK — A greyish brown colour, with red eyes.

CHOCOLATE — A dark chocolate colour with black eyes and dark grey ears.

ROAN OR SILVER — A white animal evenly ticked with darker hairs all over the body, to give a sort of mottled appearance. Can be distinguished from the Dominant Spot by the fact that the Roan has no solid spots, more "splashes" of colour. Roan is closely related to the white bellied gene.

WHITE BELLIED — Seems to be able to occur in most colours, but perhaps most common

A female long haired Rex Golden Umbrous Banded. The umbrous, or sooty, gene darkens the golden color. Note the dark gray crescents that normally would be almost white.

are White Bellied Goldens. A White Bellied Hamster has a pure white belly, and the crescents are a much more brilliant white than those of an ordinary colour such as a Golden. A ruby sheen can be seen to the eyes. Two White Bellied Hamsters must never be mated together, as this mating will produce eyeless white hamsters — pure white hamsters, about one in four of which may be born without eyes.

UMBROUS (Sooty) — This is a gene that darkens colour. An Umbrous Golden Hamster will be very dark grey on the back, with a grey belly and grey crescent. Similarly, an Umbrous Cinnamon will have a grey tinge and grey belly and crescents. When combining the umbrous gene with the black eyed cream, sable will result.

BANDED DOMINANT SPOT — This is simply a combination of the Banded and the Dominant Spot. The hamster is white with coloured spots but has a more or less clear area of white in the middle of the body. Obviously, it is rather difficult to distinguish a white band on a mainly white body. The easiest way to tell

whether a hamster is a Banded Dominant Spot or just a plain Dominant Spot is by mating it to a self-coloured animal such as a Golden. A Dominant Spot will then give Dominant Spot and self coloured babies, whereas a Banded Dominant Spot will throw both Dominant Spot, Banded, Self and Banded Dominant Spot.

BLACK — This is a very exciting new colour: a true black. The hamster is jet black with no light eye circles as in the sable. When it gets older, however, it may get a brown tinge. Black is a completely new gene, which is expected to lead to the development of a great many new colours. It was introduced into Britain as late as 1990. I saw it for the first time whilst judging in Finland in 1986. At this time, the

The dominant spot gene dilutes the color of the hamster, thus making the cinnamon color of this animal very pale.

A rather pale Cream Hamster nibbling on a treat.

Black Hamster was completely unknown in England. The Finnish breeders told me that they had acquired their animals from France. In 1987 the Blacks were imported into Sweden and then later from Sweden to England.

SILVER GREY — This is a colour which, at its best, is a nice silver coloured animal. At its worst, it can be very easy to confuse with a light grey. Not a great deal is, as yet, known about this variety. It was imported to Sweden from Holland in 1986. The gene seems to be responsible for diluting some colours, such as cream. When crossing Cream to Silver Grey, "off-white" babies will result. The colour arrived in England at the same time the Blacks arrived — 1990.

DARK EARED BLACK EYED WHITE — This is a black eyed white hamster with dark, nearly black, ears. It was originally found in litters bred from Silver Greys.

TORTOISESHELL (no white) — This hamster is the same as the Tortoiseshell and White, only without the white. A Tortoiseshell without white will usually have smaller patches of colour than one with white, and it is not quite as effective.

"TRUE" CHOCOLATE — This variety was discovered when breeding of the Black was being undertaken. It is a product of a cross between Black and Rust, unlike the original Chocolate, which is produced by crossing Sable and Rust. Its shade of colour can vary, from darkest plain Chocolate

The Silver Grey, another new variety. This colour can have many different shades. This particular hamster has a nice colour but is slightly pale, and the cheekflashes are not dark enough.

to palest Milk.

DOVE — This is a very attractive, even silvery grey colour with red eyes. Genetically it is a diluted version of the Black. It is produced by crossing Black with Cinnamon.

SILVERED BLACK — This is really a White Bellied Black. When the White bellied gene is put onto a Black, the effect will be quite stunning. The animal will be jet black with large patches of white on its belly, and an even white ticking over the entire body.

HAMSTER CLUBS AND SOCIETIES AROUND THE WORLD

The hamster fancy started in Britain but is now spreading across the world. More and more countries are forming clubs and holding shows. As most clubs change

their address (because of changes of secretaries or officers) from time to time, it is not practical to list these addresses in a book. If you do want to locate the club in your country, please write to me care of:

TFH Publications
P O Box 15
Waterlooville
PO7 6BQ
England

Please enclose a stamped self-addressed envelope or International Reply Coupon as appropriate.

The very first hamster club to be formed was the British Hamster Club, formed in 1945. This was later split into area clubs around the country, with the national club as a sort of governing body. BHC was later replaced by the National Syrian Hamster Council. In 1992

Judging of the long haired male class at a British hamster show.

the British Hamster Association was formed as an alternative to the National Syrian Hamster Council. The BHA caters for all species of hamster, not just the Syrians. Both of the national bodies have area clubs, and you can join the one that is most conveniently located for you.

The second hamster club in the world was probably the Swedish Hamster Society— Svenska Hamsterföreningen. This was formed by a handful of enthusiasts, myself included, in 1982. It was the first specialist club for small animals, other than rabbits, in Sweden, and it is still going strong today.

The hamster fancy in America has not been very strong, and it was not until 1990 that a society was formed that actually included hamsters: the American Rat, Mouse, and Hamster Association. Hopefully, it will continue to grow.

The only other countries that I know of with any sort of organised hamster fancies are Holland and Finland. They, however, do not have specialist clubs, but the hamsters are catered for within collective clubs for all sorts of small animals.

HAMSTER SHOWS

If you have decided that you want to show your hamster or hamsters, the first thing to do is either to join the nearest hamster club or to get in touch with the club secretary to find out where and when the nearest show will be held. You can always go along just to look, or bring a hamster if you like. You do not have to join the fancy to be allowed to show. Should you like showing, you can always join after the show. There are, however, many good reasons for joining the

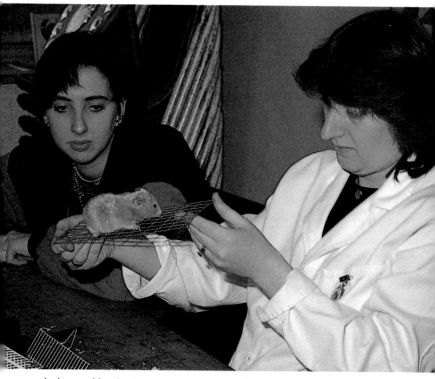

Judge and book steward during proceedings at a British hamster show.

fancy even if you do *not* want to show. For example, when joining a hamster club, you will receive a club journal, and that can be very useful. You can read interesting articles, tips, and stories about hamsters, as well as show results and judges' comments.

ENTERING YOUR HAMSTER

When you have found out where and when the next show will be, it will be time to decide which hamster or hamsters to enter, and in what classes. If you are not sure whether your hamster is of good show quality or not, or if you perhaps do not know what colour it is, it may be a good idea to enter it in the pet class the very first time. In that class the hamsters are judged on tameness and condition only. Once at the show, you can ask the more experienced exhibitors about your hamster and find out if it is of show quality. Perhaps at the next show you may then want to enter it in its breed class.

Most likely you will have been given a show schedule by the show secretary when you made your inquiries. This schedule will tell you all the relevant details about the show: times, places, directions, etc., as well as a list of classes, how much the entry fee is, when the entry has to be made, and what prizes are on offer. A typical listing of classes may look like this:

Straight Classes:
1. Golden
2. Cream
3. White
4. Cinnamon
5. AOC (any other colours)
6. Satin
7. Long haired male
8. Long haired female
9. Long haired satin
Classes 1-9 to include rex.

Duplicate Classes:
10. Junior male

Even if your hamster is not of show quality, you can still enter him in a show—in the pet class.

11. Junior female
12. Novice
13. Breeders
14. Supporters
15. Grand challenge

Other Classes:
16. Pets
17. Non-standard

How do you know what classes to enter? Well, that depends on a few things. The first thing you must remember is always to enter a straight class. You cannot enter any duplicate classes if you have not entered the straight class first. Let's say that you want to enter a short haired dark Golden. You will then enter it in class Number 1, Golden. That is the only straight class in which you can enter it.

A long haired Lilac Hamster.

The junior classes are for exhibitors aged 16 years and under. The sexes refer to the sex of the hamster, not the owner. Therefore, if you are under 16, and if your hamster is a female, you will be eligible to enter it into class number 11, Junior female.

If you are new to showing, you will probably be eligible for entry in class 12, Novice. In this instance a novice is any person who has not yet won two first prizes in classes of seven or more hamsters. Class 13, Breeders, is a class you can enter if you have

Any hamster that is to be shown should be in the peak of good health.

A hamster investigating its food bowl.

bred your hamster yourself. Class 14, Supporters, is for the benefit of the club that is staging the show. No prize money will be given, only cards, and all proceeds from the class will go to the club. Class number 15 is the Grand Challenge. This is where all the hamsters will compete for the top awards, like Best in Show and Best Opposite Sex. You should always enter

If you are going to give your hamster toys of this design, make sure they are large enough for him to climb through with ease.

bred the hamster yourself), 14 and 15. Of course, you do not *have to* enter all these classes. Classes 1 and 15 will do just as well. However, it does not cost much to enter each class, and it is usually worth entering as many classes as possible. After all, the more classes you enter, the more cards you can win! Class 16 is for pet hamsters only, and they cannot be entered into any other class. The same goes for class 17, Non-standard. A non-standard hamster can only be entered into this one class.

SHOW PENS

this class. So, let's say that you are 15 years old with a female Golden Hamster. This is your first show. You can then enter into classes number 1, 11, 12, 13 (if you have

All hamsters at shows have to be in special show pens. The pens, made of wood, are built to specific measurements. They are white on the inside, black

A long haired Pale Eared White Hamster (albino).

on the outside. Show pens can usually be bought from someone within the hamster club. Sometimes they are ready made, and sometimes they are in the form of a kit to assemble and then paint. It may also be possible to buy show pens secondhand from somebody who may be giving up showing hamsters. If you are not sure whether you would like to go on showing hamsters, or if you cannot get hold of any show pens before the show, it is a good idea to hire show pens to begin with. You are usually able to hire up to three show pens per show at a nominal cost. Remember that "first come is first served" and, as each club only has a certain number of hire pens, make sure to book yours early. Details of this will be found in the show schedule. The show pen must not be marked in any way to distinguish you as the owner. It must look the same as all the others. The only mark of identification that is allowed is a small label with your name and address *underneath* the pen. Short haired hamsters should have wood shavings in their show pens, and long haired hamsters should have cat litter of the wood-based type that looks rather like pellets. No other materials are allowed. Every now and then, you will need to repaint your show pens. Remember to use *glossy* black and white paints. The white colour will often go yellow with age, and it may start to flake. As a judge is allowed to

A pretty, bright-eyed Golden Dominant Spot Hamster.

deduct some points if the show pen is in bad condition, do not risk this. Repaint when necessary. Always make sure that you use a non-toxic paint.

SHOW PREPARATIONS FOR YOUR HAMSTER

A hamster does not need a lot of preparation for a show. It does not need any kind of trimming of the coat, nor should it have a bath. You can, however, carefully brush the coat of a long haired with a toothbrush, and perhaps polish the fur of a short haired or satin with a piece of cloth. Before you put the long haired hamster inside the show pen, make sure that its

A hamster savouring one of several types of compressed-seed treats that are produced for hamsters.

Female long haired Satin Cream Hamster.

coat is free from any sawdust or woodshavings, and free of knots. Check your hamster's nails. If they are over-long, cut them. That is all that needs to be done, apart from perhaps the most important factor: make sure that your hamster is in good health and *tame*! No judge likes to handle a skittish hamster that has not been tamed, and he may disqualify it if it is too difficult to handle. It is no use showing very young hamsters. In some countries, such as Sweden, young hamsters compete in their own classes and not against the adults, but in Britain all ages compete against each other. A young hamster will not be grown and mature enough to compete with adults, so leave that one at home until it is older.

ON THE SHOW DAY

When you travel to the show, make sure that your hamsters are comfortable. They must not get too cold in the winter or too hot in the summer. On arrival at the show, the first thing you should do is to see the show secretary. He or she will give you your pen labels and charge you for your entries. This business done, you can unpack your hamsters and check that all is well. Fasten the correct pen label on the correct show pen. (If you do not have your own, you will have collected your hire pens at the same time that you collected your labels). The sticky label should be stuck onto the top left-hand corner of the show pen. Nothing must be written by you on this label. All you have to do now is to place your hamsters on the table and wait for the judging to start. It is probably best just to watch the very first time, but if you want to get involved later on, you can ask to do something useful, such as serve as a pen steward. As an exhibitor, you will not be allowed to watch the judging, except from a

A long haired Satin Dark Grey male. Long haired males always have longer fur than do females.

Diet is an important influence in your hamster's overall appearance.

comments written on it. This is very helpful. At other shows, this system may not be in use. The judge will then note down on the pen label the number of points that the hamster gained. A small round sticker will indicate that the hamster has won a prize. Red stands for first, blue for second, yellow for third and green for fourth. The judge will work through the hamsters, one by one, class by class. It is quite a task, and the judge is certainly doing his or her best to be as quick as possible, so do try not to be impatient! Talk to people instead and enjoy yourself. The judge will remove each hamster from its show pen and place it on a small square of wire. This is so that he can look at the hamster from all angles, including

distance. You can, however, look at all the entered hamsters on the table, and you will also be able to see how they are placed. At some shows, each hamster is given a judging sheet, with points and

Do not let your hamster be subject to stress prior to the show day or on the actual show day itself: stick to his regular routines as much as possible.

underneath, with as little disturbance as possible. Most often the hamsters will be judged under a lamp fitted with a daylight bulb. This is to make sure that all hamsters are judged under the same appropriate light. The judge will go over the hamster point by point, and his book steward will write the points down for him on the judging sheets, together with any comments. The pen steward or stewards will bring the hamsters to the judging table in their show pens, usually one class at a time. When a class has been judged, the winner is the hamster with the highest number of points. Similarly, the winner of the Best in Show award is the hamster with the highest number of points in the show. At most shows, a Best Opposite Sex is also selected. If the BIS is a male, the BOS will be the best female in the show. A Best in Show junior and Best Opposite Sex junior will be selected in the same way. When the show is over, you can collect your hamsters from the table and also collect any cards and prize money that you may have been lucky enough to win. If your hamster has won a first prize, it will probably receive a rosette and a trophy, which will be presented at the prize ceremony. If you have any queries about your hamsters or about the way they were judged, approach the judge *after* the show. He will probably be more than happy to explain the judging results to you. Well, that's it. That's hamster showing. Simple, and a lot of fun! Don't take it *too* seriously though...It is only a hobby after all!

Opposite page: Profile study of a hamster. Showing hamsters is not the costly venture that holds true for many other types of pet.

Syrian Hamsters are friendly, lovable little animals, and their appeal is ever growing in the world of small pets.

Miscellaneous Tips

THE HAMSTER ON HOLIDAY

Many parents' argument for *not* getting a pet is "What will we do with it when we go on holiday?". However, this does not necessarily have to be a problem with such a small and easy-to-look-after animal as a hamster. Consider the following options:

•Perhaps the hamster can come with you? A single hamster in its cage does not take up much space. Do check, though,

When travelling with your hamster, don't forget to bring along the basic necessities of food, water, and wood shavings.

that pets are welcome at the hotel or wherever you are going. And do not forget to bring plenty of supplies for the hamster, such as food and wood shavings. If you travel by car, make sure that the hamster does not get too hot or is in a draft.

•Have you a friend or a relative that can look after the hamster while you are away?

•If no friend or relative is available, your pet shop may very well board it for you. Check well in advance, as they may be fully booked early on if you are going away at a typical holiday season

Someone or something has caught the attention of this little fellow. A tractable hand-tame hamster is a pleasure to own.

such as summer or Christmas.

• If you are only going to be away for a weekend, it is possible to leave the hamster at home with no one looking after it. Just make sure that there is plenty of food and clean water for the hamster and that the cage is absolutely escape proof.

BEWARE OF...

A hamster is a very small animal, and it can easily get hurt by objects that may seem to be perfectly safe. Beware of the following:

• Do not give your hamster a very tall cage, such as a bird cage or a two-storey cage. If the hamster falls from the top, it may hurt itself very badly, perhaps even die.

• If you build your own hamster cage, make sure

Hamsters are active pets that enjoy exploring their environment.

that the mesh you use is very fine, approximately 1cm x 1cm square. Bigger mesh and especially chicken wire can be a great danger to the hamster. In an attempt to escape, he may get his head stuck. Young babies may be able to escape.

•If you let your hamster occasionally run free on the floor, do make sure that there are no electrical cables that the hamster can chew. Also check that there are no small holes in the wall or the floor boards that the hamster can get through.

•If you use exercise wheels for your hamsters, you may want to remove them when the females have young. A baby can easily get hurt when the mother uses the wheel.

•Never keep a hamster's cage close to a window. It will get too hot in the summer, too cold in the winter, and the draft can cause eye problems and colds.

•Never use cotton wool as a nesting material for hamsters. A hamster can easily get its legs stuck in it and can also suffocate if it puts the material in its cheek pouches.

•Never use hay as nesting material. Sharp straws can damage a hamster's eyes or cheek pouches. Even soft shredded tissue should be avoided as nesting material for long haired hamsters as there have been instances of injury resulting from the tissue becoming entangled in the long fur.

IF THE HAMSTER ESCAPES

Hamsters are clever little animals, and if the cage is not perfectly escape proof, you can rest assured that, sooner or later, the hamster will find its way out. If this

If you are going to let your hamster run free, it is best to confine it to one room. Additionally, make sure there are no safety hazards to which it could be exposed.

happens, you may have a problem on your hands. The hamster is gone, and you cannot find it! If the door to the room where the hamster's cage was kept was open, the hamster could by now be anywhere in the house. The first thing to do is to find which room the hamster is hiding in. This is most easily done by closing all doors in

Black Eyed Cream Hamster.

room to see if any of the food has been touched. If it has, you know in which room the hamster is. If you know in which room the hamster is, but still cannot find it or catch it, it may be a good idea to set a trap. You can make a safe trap yourself by the use of a bucket, some books and some hamster food. Put the bucket, with food inside, in the middle of the floor. By the side of the bucket you build "steps," with the help of the books. Now the hamster can smell the food in the bucket and will be able to climb up to the top. Most likely it will then fall down into the bucket and will not be able to climb back out again. This is usually very effective!

the house. In each room put a small quantity of food on the floor. After a few hours, check every

Dwarf Hamsters

Dwarf hamsters have become increasingly popular during the last few years. There are several different species from which to chose, and more and more colour variations are being developed all the time. (There is, however, still a long way to go until the same choice of colors that is available in the Syrian Hamster becomes available in dwarf hamsters.) A dwarf hamster is a delightful little creature, which usually makes just as good a pet as the Syrian Hamster. Remember, though, that with their minute size, only about a third that of the Syrian Hamster, they may be difficult for young

A Pearl Winter White Russian Dwarf Hamster.

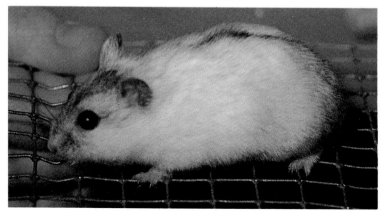

children to handle. They are also slightly more difficult to breed than the Syrian Hamster. There are three varieties of dwarf hamsters that are commonly being kept as pets or show animals.

They are the Chinese Hamster, Campbell's Russian Hamster, and the Winter White Russian Hamster. Their looks do differ, but all of them measure about 7 centimetres long as

This photo gives a good indication of just how small a dwarf hamster is.

A pair of Normal Coloured Chinese Hamsters.

adults. Their care differs slightly from that of the Syrian Hamster, but many aspects are similar. For example, their feeding is identical to that of the Syrian Hamster. Many aspects of caring for dwarf hamsters can, therefore, be found by reading the chapters about the Syrian Hamster in this book.

THE CHINESE HAMSTER
(Cricetulus griseus)

The Chinese Hamster differs slightly in looks from the other dwarf species kept as pets. The Chinese is a fairly long and thin hamster. It has feet very much like the Syrian Hamster, with sparse fur. Its tail is slightly longer than that of a Syrian Hamster, making it a bit mouse-like in appearance. As yet, the Chinese Hamster only comes in two colour variations. Its natural colour is brown, with a dark stripe along the spine and a white belly. The Dominant Spot Chinese Hamster exhibits a pattern similar to that of the Syrian Hamster. It is white, with large and small patches of the normal colour. Usually, the Dominant Spot Chinese has a white head spot. It is possible to breed a Dominant Spot Chinese "without the spots," i.e., generation by generation reduce the number of coloured spots, until at last all that remains is a pure white body with black eyes. This is, however, still extremely rare. It is difficult to tell for certain whether a Chinese Hamster will make a good pet. Ask ten different people, and you will get ten different answers! My own personal experience is that the Chinese is difficult to tame and can sometimes be hard to handle at all. Other people will tell you that their Chinese are very nice and tame, and I have indeed seen very friendly Chinese Hamsters. Among all the dwarf varieties, there seem to be different strains with different behaviour. One breeder may produce lots of friendly Chinese that are easy to handle, whereas another may only produce babies that are very difficult to tame. It is important, therefore, that you find a breeder who has nice, friendly animals if it is a pet hamster that you are looking for.

A Dominant Spot Chinese Hamster.

DWARF RUSSIAN HAMSTERS

The two Dwarf Russian Hamsters do at first glance look very similar, but after a closer look you will realise that they are slightly different. In fact, they are two different species. It is not possible to breed Campbell's Russian (*Phodopus sungoris campbelli*) and a Winter White Russian (*Phodopus sungoris sungoris*) together, just as it is not possible to breed, for example, a Chinese to a Syrian.

Two young Campbell's Russians: a Normal Coloured and an Albino.

A Normal Coloured Campbell's Dwarf Russian Hamster.

Campbell's Russian Hamster

Campbell's Russian is the slightly larger of the two Russian Hamsters. It is a round, furry hamster. Its face is fairly blunt, and the body is much more rounded than that of the Chinese. It has a lot of fur on all of its feet and on its tail. In fact, it is sometimes referred to as the "furry-footed hamster." The tail is very short.

Campbell's Russian

A pretty Banded Campbell's Dwarf Russian Hamster.

can be found in a number of colour variations. The normal-coloured Campbell's Russian has a colour very similar to that of the normal-coloured Chinese. It is brown with a dark stripe along its spine and has a white belly. The first mutation to appear in Campbell's Russian was that of the satin coat. The hamster's coat is very glossy and shiny, rather like the satin version of the Syrian Hamster. However, in the case of Campbell's Russian, the fur has something of a "wet" look, and it does not work in the same way genetically as the Syrian version. To produce a satin-coated Campbell's, you need to mate together either two satins, one satin and a carrier (a normal-coated hamster bred from a satin), or two carriers.

Campbell's Russian also comes in an albino variety. This hamster is pure white with pink eyes. It looks like a little cotton ball and is most attractive! Exciting new varieties are the Banded and Dominant Spot, often collectively referred to as the "Mottled" variety. Not much is yet known about these two varieties, which

Two young Albino Campbell's Dwarf Russian Hamsters.

seem to be closely related. The Banded Campbell's has a white band rather like the white-banded Syrian, but the band is generally located around the hamster's neck rather than the waist. White spots may appear on the body. The Dominant Spot, or Piebald, as it is also known, has varying degrees of white spots on the body.

The final colour variation is the Cinnamon, also called the Argente. This colour looks somewhat similar

The newest colour variety of Campbell's Russian: the Banded.

An Albino Campbell's Dwarf Russian Hamster.

to that of the Cinnamon Syrian Hamster. The fur is of an orange shade, the eyes are red, and the belly fur white. This variety is still very rare.

Just as with the Chinese Hamster, some people will tell you that Campbell's Russian Hamsters make good pets; others will say that they do not. You can find both friendly and unfriendly examples of Campbell's, so take care when making your choice.

The Winter White Russian Hamster

The Winter White Russian Hamster is a fascinating little creature. It is slightly smaller than its cousin Campbell's Russian Hamster, with a slightly more blunt face. Otherwise, the looks are the same, with the furry feet and the short tail. The reason why this variety is called "winter white" is, simply, that in its natural colour, the hamster is able to turn almost pure white in the wintertime...Rather like certain species of hare! The hamster will only go white, however, if kept in fairly cool conditions, such as in a shed. If it is kept in a centrally heated room, it will keep its

A baby Winter White Russian Dwarf Hamster of the original (or normal) colour.

A Winter White Russian Dwarf Hamster. This species is a bit smaller than its cousin Campbell's Dwarf Russian.

natural colour all year 'round. This can actually be rather useful, as a Winter White Russian in its winter coat will *not* breed. The Winter White Russian comes in three colour varieties. The natural colour is a silvery grey colour, with a dark stripe down its spine and a pure white belly. When the hamster turns white in the winter, the fur will go almost pure white but will still retain the dark stripe. The Pearl is a beautiful colour variety of the Winter White, perhaps the most striking of all the dwarf varieties. It is very similar to the colour of a normal Winter White in its winter coat. The fur is white with a black stripe down the spine, and some or all of the hairs are delicately ticked with black. A curious fact about these beautiful animals is that all the male pearls appear to be sterile. This is not a problem, though, as the colour is dominant, and you will get both pearls and normals by mating a normal male to a Pearl female.

The third colour of the Winter White is the Sapphire, a paler bluish grey colour with a grey stripe down the spine and

A Sapphire Winter White Russian Dwarf Hamster.

a white belly. This is still a rare variety, as is the Pearl, although both are becoming more and more popular. My own personal experience is, that of the dwarf hamsters commonly kept as pets, it is the Winter White Russian that has the best temperament. They are very friendly and easy to handle, and I have never come across a Winter White that did not tame quickly. They are truly delightful little animals.

Roborovski's Dwarf Hamster, the newest type of dwarf hamster to be kept as a pet.

OTHER DWARF HAMSTERS

The dwarf hamsters discussed above are by no means all of the varieties of dwarf hamster that exist. There are several more. The only other one that, so far, is being kept as a pet is Roborovski's Dwarf Hamster. It is a brown colour, similar to the Russian in build but lacking the black stripe down the spine. It does exist in England, but it is still very, very rare. Roborovski's Hamster is smaller than the other dwarf varieties. It tends to be very lively and, therefore, difficult to handle.

Dwarf hamsters like houses in which they can sleep and nest.

Care of the Dwarf Varieties

As mentioned earlier, much of the care of the dwarf hamsters is similar to that of the Syrian Hamster. I will mention here, therefore, only those matters that are different.

DWARFS ARE KEPT IN PAIRS

The single most significant difference between the Syrian Hamster and the dwarf hamster is that dwarf hamsters are kept in pairs. A single dwarf is not a very happy hamster. The best option is, of course, to keep a pair consisting of a male and a female. They will live happily together all their life. Naturally, a true pair will breed, and they will look after the babies together. If you do not want to breed, chose two males or two females. They will also live happily together. The males are usually more placid and friendly, so perhaps two males is a better choice than two females. Dwarf hamsters pair for life. They should be kept together at all times. It is usually not possible to change one of the partners for another after they have been together for a while. Dwarfs need to be paired up at a young age, preferably at 4 to 12 weeks. Later on, it can be very difficult to get a dwarf to accept a partner. Obviously, accidents do happen, and you may find yourself, for example, with a single male after a female has died. You can then *carefully* try to introduce a new partner to him.

It is usually much easier to introduce a new female to an older male, than vice versa. It is also easier to introduce a youngster to an adult, rather than adult to adult. Clean out the older hamster's cage completely or, even better, change it for another cage. Try making the two hamsters smell of the same scent. You can, for example, put a small dab of perfume on each hamster's back. In this way, they will both have a similar smell, and the newcomer may not instantly be recognised as a stranger. Start by putting the two hamsters together in a neutral area, such as a box. If everything seems fine, put them together in the cage and hope for the best. Generally, it is impossible to introduce a new male to a single Chinese female, whereas it may work with the Russians.

THE CAGE

The cage for a pair of dwarf hamsters must be very escape proof. Such small hamsters can squeeze through almost anything, so a normal hamster cage will not do. The bars are too far apart. A good choice is an aquarium with a very fine mesh lid, or perhaps a plastic box, again with a mesh lid. The size of the cage should, preferably, be larger than the cage for a Syrian Hamster, perhaps 40cm x 40cm.

This large plastic tank makes an ideal cage for a pair of dwarf hamsters.

Dwarfs like space, and remember that if you have a breeding pair, there may be a lot of hamsters in the cage at times. Just as would be provided for Syrians, use wood shavings as bedding. Sawdust is too fine and can prove dangerous. Nesting material is optional but,

Dwarf hamsters usually love exercise wheels, so it is a good idea to get them one. Any type will do, and they can be of the smallest kind available. Cardboard rolls will be much appreciated to play in, especially by youngsters.

Most dwarf hamsters like to have a house or nest box. As they are such small animals, the plastic and wooden houses available in pet shops will do nicely. An alternative to a house is the shell of half a coconut, with a little door made in one side. In fact, many dwarfs like to have two houses. If the female has recently given birth, she may not allow the male in the nest with her, and he will then appreciate a "spare" house to sleep in.

The smallest kind of exercise wheel available will do just fine for dwarf hamsters.

if used, should be of the shredded paper kind. A bowl for food and one for water (if it is not possible to fit a bottle into the cage) is, of course, essential.

Breeding Dwarf Hamsters

Breeding dwarf hamsters is both easier and more difficult than breeding Syrian Hamsters. You do not need to bother to mate the hamsters, and find which day the female is on heat, as the hamsters will do this themselves, living together all the time. On the other hand, they may not always breed when you want them to, or they may even breed *too* much. Once you have decided that you *do* want to breed

A pair of Campbell's Dwarf Russian Hamsters mating.

dwarf hamsters, select a young pair. The pair should be approximately of the same age. Littermates will do nicely. All you will need to do now is to leave the hamsters living together, and let them get on with it. With any luck, they will start to breed as soon as they feel ready. How long this takes varies. Some pairs will start to breed at the age of four months. Others will wait for six to eight months, and others will never breed at all.

The female dwarf

Campbell's Dwarf Russian Hamster, shown here a few days old. The stripe down the spine, characteristic of most dwarf species, is clearly visible.

A Campbell's Dwarf Russian Hamster at two weeks of age. Dwarf hamsters develop very quickly.

hamster is pregnant for 16 to 18 days. She will then give birth, usually, to two to six babies. She normally is a very good mother, and the male will help her to look after the babies. The babies develop much the same as Syrian babies, perhaps slightly quicker. At the age of three to four weeks, at the latest, they are ready to leave their parents. Some female dwarfs have litters very regularly. It is possible for a female dwarf to produce a litter every 16 days. In this case, her older babies must be removed by the age of 16 days, as soon as the new litter is born, or the new litter may be killed. It is more common,

This Winter White Russian Dwarf Hamster has made an empty plant pot his house.

however, that the female produces a litter once a month or, perhaps, only once every two months. She decides herself when she wants to breed and will take a break when she feels tired. There is no need, therefore, to be worried that she is breeding too much. She knows what is best for her.

As mentioned earlier, Winter White Russians in their winter coats will not breed. Chinese Hamsters will need to be kept slightly cooler than other dwarfs to be able to breed. This is because the male's testicles are unusually large. They need to be kept cool to be able to produce sperm that is fertile.

Pearl female and Normal Winter White Russian Dwarf male with their two-week-old Pearl offspring. All male Pearls are sterile so a Pearl female must always be mated to a Normal Coloured male.

Health Care for Dwarf Hamsters

Dwarf hamsters are very hardy little animals, and they hardly ever become ill. Usually they stay healthy during their entire life, which normally is between 18 months and 2 years. They do, however, commonly suffer from two conditions in old age. The first one is cataracts. The hamster's eyes will go grey or almost white, and the hamster will be blind. This condition is common and cannot be cured. The hamster will probably be fairly old and may not have many months left to live. Let it live the rest of its life as normal. It will not suffer.

The other condition common in older dwarfs is cancer. Tumours may appear anywhere on the body. Cancer is also basically impossible to cure. It is far too difficult to operate on an animal of such small size. Let the hamster live for as long as it does not suffer. When the tumours start to hurt the hamster or grow so large as to cause discomfort, have the hamster put to sleep.

Opposite page: A Winter White Russian Dwarf Hamster that has just started to change into its paler winter coat.

A pair of Winter White Russian Dwarf Hamsters. The female is in her beautiful winter coat.

Showing Dwarf Hamsters

Showing dwarf hamsters is fairly similar to showing Syrian Hamsters. Some things do vary, of course, such as the look of the official show pen. Additionally, with dwarfs, it is possible to show two animals in each pen. Shows for dwarf hamsters are not as common as those for Syrian Hamsters. They do exist though, so contact your nearest hamster club to find out the details. In Britain, we have an organisation called G.O.S.H. (Group for Other Species of Hamster), and this body regularly organises shows for dwarf hamsters. The British Hamster Association is also staging shows for dwarf hamsters. Both clubs share the same exhibition standards (originally laid down by G.O.S.H.). The different standards published by the BHA in April 1992 are as follows:

CAMPBELL'S RUSSIAN HAMSTER

Colour: The top coat shall be a brownish-buffish grey to ochre grey, with a slate blue undercoat. The belly fur shall be whitish with a heavy blue-grey undercolour. The feet are white.

Type and Build: The build shall be likened to a bullet, roundish in shape, the legs shall be short and scarcely visible.

Fur: The fur shall be dense with a very thick undercoat. The entire coat and undercoat to give a wooly impression.

Head, Eyes, Ears, and Legs: The head shall be short and broad with noticeable cheeks. The round eyes must not bulge and shall be black in colour. The ears shall be small and round yet show above the fur, the insides shall be a little hairy. The soles of the hind feet shall have dense fur.

Size: An adult shall have an ideal length of approximately 7cm.

Markings: The boundary between the belly and the top colour shall be formed by three prominently marked arches. The colour of the arches shall be dark buff to black. A dark black stripe shall run from between the eyes, down the back to the tail.

Condition: The hamster shall have a lively image with clear bright eyes.

Minor Faults: Small deviation in type, build and size. Slight moulting and colour

Some Pearl Russians are so pale in colour that they totally lack the dark spinal stripe.

deviation. Thin fur and short stripe.

Major Faults: Large deviation in type, build and size. Heavy moulting and thin fur. Partial or total lack of stripe. Sick, bald, wounded or pregnant animals.

CAMPBELL'S ALBINO RUSSIAN HAMSTER

Colour: The entire coat shall be pure white to the roots, devoid of any shading or marking.

Type and Build: The build shall be likened to a bullet, roundish in shape, the legs shall be short and scarcely visible.

Fur: The fur shall be dense with a very thick undercoat. The entire coat and undercoat to give a wooly impression.

Head, Eyes, Ears, and Legs: The head shall be short and broad with noticeable cheeks. The round eyes must not bulge and shall be bright clear pink in colour. The ears shall be flesh coloured, small and round, yet show above the fur, the insides shall be a little hairy. The soles of the hind feet shall have dense fur.

Size: An adult shall have an ideal

	length of approximately 7cm.
Markings:	None.
Condition:	The hamster shall have a lively image with clear bright eyes.
Minor Faults:	Small deviation in type, build and size. Slight moulting, thin fur.

A Campbell's Dwarf Russian Hamster getting its daily exercise.

Major Faults: Large deviation in type, build and size. Heavy moulting and thin fur. Sick, bald, wounded or pregnant animals. Dirty or stained fur shall be heavily penalised.

SATIN CAMPBELL'S RUSSIAN HAMSTER

Colour and markings shall be as for existing varieties (i.e., Albino, normal) allowing for satinisation. The fur shall be extremely fine and glossy, giving a somewhat less dense appearance.

WINTER WHITE RUSSIAN HAMSTER

Colour: The top coat shall be grey-brown to ochre grey, with a slate blue undercoat. The belly fur must be clean white, the undercoat to be slightly tinged with a little blue. The feet are white.

NB: With winter day length, the colour moults to a complete white with the exception of the dorsal stripe. A show animal should show no signs of moult.

Type and Build: The build shall be likened to a bullet, roundish in shape, the legs should be short and the tail very short and scarcely visible.

Fur: The fur shall be dense with a very thick undercoat. The entire coat

An adult Sapphire Winter White Russian Dwarf Hamster.

and undercoat to give a wooly impression.

Head, Eyes, Ears, and Legs:

The head shall be short and broad with noticeable cheeks. The round eyes must not bulge, black in colour. The ears shall be small and round, the insides shall be a little hairy. The soles of the hind feet shall have dense fur.

Size:

An adult shall have an ideal length of approximately 7cm.

Markings:

The boundary between the belly and top colour shall be formed by three prominently marked arches. A dark brown stripe shall run from between the eyes, down the back to the tail.

Condition:

The hamster shall have a lively image with clear bright eyes.

Minor Faults:

Small deviation in type, build and size. Slight moulting and colour deviation. Thin fur and short stripe.

Major Faults:

Large deviation in type, build and size. Heavy moulting and thin fur. Sick, bald, wounded or pregnant animals. Partial or total lack of stripe.

A pair of Roborovski's Dwarf Hamsters. Note the absence of the spinal stripe that is present in the other dwarf hamster varieties.

CHINESE HAMSTER (NORMAL COATED)

Colour:	The top colour shall be a brownish grey to yellowish ochre with a dark slate blue base colour. The belly fur shall be a beige/white with a dark blue base colour.
Type and Build:	The build shall be long and slender. The legs shall be short and the tail long.
Fur:	The fur shall be short and dense.
Head, Eyes, Ears and Legs:	The head shall be as triangular as possible. The round eyes must not over bulge, black in colour. The ears shall be small and round, blackish-brown in colour, the rim of the ears shall be lightly coloured to cream white. The feet shall be haired and white in colour, the nails shall be neutral.
Size:	An adult shall have an ideal size of approximately 3-4 inches.
Markings:	Between the back and belly fur shall be a well defined straight line from the nose, over the cheeks and along the sides. The dorsal stripe shall be regular from between the eyes to the tail.
Condition:	The hamster must show a lively

A pair of Normal Coloured Chinese Dwarf Hamsters. These animals have rather long, thin bodies.

	image with clear bright eyes.
Minor Faults:	Small deviation in type, build and size. Slight moulting and colour deviation. Thin fur and short stripe.
Major Faults:	Large deviation in type, build and size. Heavy moulting and thin fur. Partial or total lack of stripe. Sick, bald, wounded, scarred or pregnant animals.

CHINESE HAMSTER (DOMINANT SPOT)

Colour:	The top colour shall be a brownish grey to yellowish ochre with a dark slate blue base colour, both top and base colour may be broken by a varying amount of white spots or patches. The distribution of these white patches shall be as even as possible. The belly fur shall be a crisp clear white.
Type and Build:	The build shall be long and slender. The legs shall be short and the tail long.
Fur:	The fur shall be short and dense.
Head, Eyes, Ears, and Legs:	The head shall be as triangular as possible. The round eyes must not over bulge, black in colour. The

ears shall be small and round, with or without light coloured patches. The feet shall be haired and white in colour, the nails shall be neutral.

Size: An adult shall have an ideal size of approximately 3-4 inches.

Markings: Between the back and belly fur shall be a well defined straight line from the nose, over the cheeks and along the sides, this stripe may be broken by white areas. The dorsal stripe, which shall run from the eyes to the tail, may also be broken by white spots or patches.

Condition: The hamster shall show a lively image with clear bright eyes.

Minor Faults: Small deviation in type, build and size. Slight moulting and colour deviation. Thin fur and short stripe.

Major Faults: Large deviation in type, build and size. Heavy moulting and thin fur. Partial or total lack of stripe. Sick, bald, wounded, scarred, or pregnant animals.

WINTER WHITE RUSSIAN HAMSTER, PEARL

Colour: The top coat shall be pure white

to the roots, lightly and evenly ticked with black guard hairs. The belly fur must be pure white.

Type and Build: The build shall be likened to a bullet, roundish in shape, the legs should be short and the tail very short and scarcely visible.

Fur: The fur shall be dense with a very thick undercoat. The entire coat and undercoat to give a wooly impression.

Head, Eyes, Ears, and Legs: The head shall be short and broad with noticeable cheeks. The round eyes must not bulge, black in colour. The ears shall be small and round, the insides shall be a little hairy. The ear colour shall be light grey ear lobe to flesh base. The soles of the hind feet shall have dense fur.

Size: An adult shall have an ideal length of approximately 7cm.

Markings: No markings must be visible.

Condition: The hamster shall have a lively image with clear bright eyes.

Minor Faults: Small deviation in type, build and size. Slight moulting and colour deviation.

Major Faults: Large deviation in type, build and

Chinese Dwarf Hamsters: Normal Coloured and Dominant Spot. A
normal hamster cage (with bars) cannot be used for dwarf hamsters
because the animals can squeeze through the bars. Instead, use an
aquarium tank or a plastic box—fitted with a very fine mesh lid.

size. Heavy moulting and thin fur.
Sick, bald, wounded, or pregnant
animals. Irregular and/or heavy
ticking, partial or total lack of
stripe shall be heavily penalised.
Dirty or stained fur shall be
heavily penalised.

WINTER WHITE RUSSIAN HAMSTER, SAPPHIRE

Colour:
The top coat shall be a soft smoky
grey with a blue tinge with a soft
dark grey undercoat. The belly fur
is white and the undercoat may
be slightly tinged with smoky
grey.

Type and Build:
The build shall be likened to a
bullet, roundish in shape, the legs
should be short and the tail very
short and scarcely visible.

Fur:
The fur shall be dense with a very
thick undercoat. The entire coat
and undercoat to give a wooly
impression.

Head, Eyes, Ears
and Legs:
The head shall be short and broad
with noticeable cheeks. The round
eyes must not bulge, black in
colour. The ears shall be small
and round, the insides shall be a
little hairy. The ear colour shall be

Dwarf hamsters come in several colour varieties, but they do not match the Syrian Hamster in the wide choice of colours in which it is available.

soft grey.

Size: An adult shall have an ideal length of approximately 7cm.

Markings: The boundary between the belly and top colour shall be formed by three prominently marked arches. A soft dark grey stripe shall run from between the eyes, down the back to the tail.

Condition: The hamster shall have a lively image with clear bright eyes.

Minor Faults: Small deviation in type, build and size. Slight moulting and colour deviation.

Major Faults: Large deviation in type, build and size. Heavy moulting and thin fur. Sick, bald, wounded, or pregnant animals. Partial or total lack of stripe shall be heavily penalised.

MARKING SCHEME

Points will be awarded as follows:

Colour	25	Size	10
Type and Build	15	Markings	10
Fur	15	Condition	10
Head, Eyes,Ears,		Minor Faults	-10 maximum
and Legs	15	Major Faults	-20 maximum

NB: Untame animals are liable for disqualification. For Albino Campbell's class, the Colour and Markings points are amalgamated.

Suggested Reading

T.F.H. Publications offers the most comprehensive selection of books dealing with hamsters. A selection of significant titles is presented below; they and many other works are available from pet shops everywhere.

**Breeding Hamsters
by Marshall E. Ostrow**
ISBN 0-86622-564-1
TFH KW-134

**Hamsters
by Percy Parslow**
ISBN 0-86622-831-4
TFH KW-015

**Hamsters: A Complete
Introduction
by Mervin F. Roberts**
ISBN 0-86622-269-3
TFH CO-020

**Hamsters as a Hobby
by G. Ovechka**
ISBN 0-86622-412-2
TFH TT-006

**Hamsters as a New Pet
by Anmarie Barrie**
ISBN 0-86622-610-9
TFH TU-003

**A Step-by-Step Book
About Dwarf Hamsters
by Chris Henwood**
ISBN 0-86622-479-3
TFH SK-040

A SAVE–OUR–PLANET BOOK
THE PROFITS GO TO CONSERVATION

HAMSTERS
. . . as a hobby

Grey Ovechka

EVERYTHING YOU NEED TO KNOW TO GET STARTED

Index